Cambrid

Elements in the Philosophy of Religion
edited by
Yujin Nagasawa
University of Birmingham

RELIGIOUS FICTIONALISM

Robin Le Poidevin
University of Leeds

CAMBRIDGE
UNIVERSITY PRESS

CAMBRIDGE
UNIVERSITY PRESS

University Printing House, Cambridge CB2 8BS, United Kingdom

One Liberty Plaza, 20th Floor, New York, NY 10006, USA

477 Williamstown Road, Port Melbourne, VIC 3207, Australia

314–321, 3rd Floor, Plot 3, Splendor Forum, Jasola District Centre, New Delhi – 110025, India

79 Anson Road, #06–04/06, Singapore 079906

Cambridge University Press is part of the University of Cambridge.

It furthers the University's mission by disseminating knowledge in the pursuit of education, learning, and research at the highest international levels of excellence.

www.cambridge.org
Information on this title: www.cambridge.org/9781108457477
DOI: 10.1017/9781108558198

© Robin Le Poidevin 2019

First published 2019

A catalogue record for this publication is available from the British Library.

ISBN 978-1-108-45747-7 Paperback
ISSN 2399-5165 (online)
ISSN 2515-9763 (print)

Religious Fictionalism

Elements in the Philosophy of Religion

DOI: 10.1017/9781108558198
First published online: April 2019

Robin Le Poidevin
University of Leeds

Author for correspondence: Robin Le Poidevin, r.d.lepoidevin@leeds.ac.uk

Abstract: This Element is an introduction to contemporary religious fictionalism, its motivation and challenges. Among the issues raised are:

- Can religion be viewed as a game of make-believe?
- In what ways does religious fictionalism parallel positions often labelled 'fictionalist' in ethics and metaphysics?
- Does religious fictionalism represent an advance over its rivals?
- Can fictionalism provide an adequate understanding of the characteristic features of the religious life, such as worship, prayer, and moral commitment?
- Does fictionalism face its own version of the problem of evil?
- Is realism about theistic (God-centred) language less religiously serious than fictionalism?

Keywords: religion, fiction, fictionalism, realism, make-believe

ISBNs: 9781108457477 (PB), 9781108558198 (OC)
ISSNs: 2399-5165 (online), 2515-9763 (print)

Contents

"I'm afraid I'm a practical man," said the doctor with gruff humour, "and I don't
bother much about religion and philosophy."
"You'll never be a practical man till you do," said Father Brown.

G. K. Chesterton, 'The Dagger with Wings', from
The Incredulity of Father Brown (1926)

Prologue

During an episode of the long-running television series *Inspector Morse*, based
on the novels of Colin Dexter, passing reference is made to the (fictional)
Bishop of Banbury. 'Oh yes,' says Morse, 'the one who doesn't believe in
God.'[1] We aren't told what the Bishop does believe, but this is clearly an ironic
reference to a phenomenon which, by the late 1980s (when the series first
started), had become familiar to the viewing public: an ordained minister who
explicitly disavows a traditional conception of talk about God as being, literally,
talk about a transcendent being, in favour of some other way of interpreting
theological language. The sources of that phenomenon within theological writings go back some time – we can trace one source to the nineteenth century in
Matthew Arnold's *Literature and Dogma*, and in the twentieth century to the
writings of theologians such as Rudolf Bultmann and Paul Tillich. Arguably, it
first came to the attention of a wider public with the publication in 1963 of
Bishop John Robinson's *Honest to God*, and again in 1984 with the BBC series
The Sea of Faith, written and presented by Don Cupitt. (And it is fair to
conjecture that Cupitt, rather than Robinson, was the model for the Bishop of
Banbury: more contemporary, more radical, and much more direct.)

The natural and inevitable reaction to a statement by a member of the clergy
to the effect that we need to replace a traditional conception of God talk is an
accusation of atheism. How, the critics exclaim, can one be both a priest and an
atheist? This Element is an attempt to answer, if not quite that question, then
ones we need to pose on the way to that question: how could God talk be
understood, if not as an expression of belief in a transcendent being? Is there a
difference between such alternative understandings on the one hand and atheism on the other? Could they be the basis of a religious or spiritual life? There
are, it turns out, many different reinterpretations, and I shall focus on one in
particular, a position that has come to be known in the philosophical literature as
religious fictionalism. As I shall present it, this is the view that language about
God (and related religious language) is best understood as concerning a fictional
world, and that engaging in such language involves engaging in make-believe.
The relative simplicity of this approach and its connection with a familiar

---

[1] *Inspector Morse: Ghost in the Machine*, Zenith Productions for Central Independent Television
(1987).

phenomenon make it, I think, an attractive one. It avoids some of the problems facing other 'non-realist' interpretations of religious language. But it also faces problems of its own, and I shall be as explicit as I can about these.This is a short Element, and brevity requires focus. I have chosen to focus particularly on one important and influential source of non-realist approaches, including fictionalism, namely Richard Braithwaite's 1955 lecture, 'An Empiricist's View of the Nature of Religious Belief'. Section 2 is a commentary on Braithwaite's discussion, and Section 3 explores at some length the fictionalist aspect of Braithwaite's view with reference to more recent literature on fictionalism, a view which has now made an appearance in several areas of philosophy.

Philosophy of religion, like many areas of the discipline, has a specialised vocabulary, including names for the various 'isms' or theories. While an over-proliferation of jargon is regrettable and to be resisted where possible, it is more helpful than otherwise to have pegs on which to hang distinctively different views so as to avoid any ambiguity. Adam needed names for the different creatures in the Garden of Eden, and we too need names to navigate this garden of the mind. So a certain amount of definition is the inevitable business of the first two sections. The point, however, is not merely to engage in what one might call intellectual botanising, or marking out an area of 'logical space', as philosophers like to put it. It is to enable us to track a position though the debate. To aid the reader, I have included at the end of this Element a glossary of the more specialist terms. And to relieve the monotony of repeated technical vocabulary, I introduce in Section 3 the fictional figures of Reginald and Fiona, who stand for two opposing views of religious language and practice.

My first attempt to articulate a fictionalist position, influenced by debates in the philosophy of science, appeared in *Arguing for Atheism* (1996). In successive papers, I have tried various ways of presenting it, and I have drawn on these in this Element, in particular 'Playing the God Game: the Perils of Religious Fictionalism', in Andrei Buckareff and Yujin Nagasawa, eds., *Alternative Conceptions of God* (Oxford University Press, 2016: 178–91). There is now a growing literature on the subject, and this seems the right time for a monograph-length treatment, if only, for the time being, a rather short one. I offer it in part as a contribution to, as well as a summary of the contemporary philosophical debate. But I hope it will also be of interest to those looking for a basis for a religious mode of existence which does not require conceptual commitments they feel unable to accept. By that, I emphatically do not mean that this Element is a 'religion made easy' primer. Religion should not be an easy thing to practice, but it is worth asking whether some of the objections raised against religion, even if they have some cogency, really are obstacles to the religious life.

The relevance of the Bishop of Banbury to the Morse episode mentioned above, incidentally, is that the Bishop is the Visitor of Courtenay College, Oxford (another fictional entity), whose role it is to choose a new Master of the College in the event that the Fellows are unable to decide. The retiring Master fears that in such an event the Visitor will foist 'some incomprehensible modern theologian' on the College. I shall just say that, in theology, one can be radical without being incomprehensible. That, at any rate, is my hope.

1 Religious Realism: the Natural View?

For if the dead rise not, then is not Christ raised:
And if Christ be not raised, your faith is in vain.

1 Corinthians 15: 16–17

1.1 Defining Religious Realism

Religious fictionalism represents a radical departure from what is widely regarded as the natural, or at least the traditional view of religion, and in particular of *theistic* religion: religion for which the notion of God is central. That view is known as *realism*. Fictionalism is by no means the only alternative to realism, but it is arguably the best alternative. Like its 'non-realist' rivals, it arose as a religiously sympathetic attempt to avoid the challenges faced by the traditional view. It makes sense, then, to set the scene by describing that traditional view.

So what is it to be a 'religious realist'? What is it being realist *about*? What is its motivation? What challenges does it face? What alternative views are there? These are the questions we will address in the first two sections.

Let's begin by setting aside the everyday connotations of the term 'realism'. In describing someone as a religious realist, we do not mean that they have a hard-headed, practical, no-nonsense, unsentimental view of religion (though the realist might not object to those epithets). The meaning that is relevant to this discussion has more in common, perhaps, with the description of an artistic style as realist: it is to do with what is being represented and the way in which it is represented.

In philosophical discussion, realism is often, and perhaps primarily, to do with a view of a particular language or discourse. Take a non-religious example. Chemists talk about 'ions' – the charged particles into which ionic compounds supposedly resolve themselves when put into solution. Take a sentence like 'This solution contains sodium and chlorine ions.' A realist about ion talk takes this sentence to have the intended function of saying something true about the world as it really is independently of whether anyone thinks it is that way. It is, as we will put it, intended to be *objectively fact-stating*. Further, the realist will deny that the facts underlying ion talk can equally well be conveyed by sentences which make no mention of ions at all – for example, sentences about the directly observable behaviour of solutions. We will express this by saying that ion talk is *irreducible* to other kinds of talk. No doubt much of scientific theory concerns what there is in the world. And we might make this the primary issue. Ian Hacking, for example, characterises scientific realism in terms of existence: '*Scientific realism* says that the entities, states and processes described by correct theories really do exist' (Hacking (1983): 21). But scientific theories also concern the *way* things are, so we might want to add to Hacking's definition 'and those entities, states and processes really are the way those correct scientific theories say they are.' Note the important qualification 'correct': it is *not* part of scientific realism that our currently scientific theories are in fact correct. The realist allows that at least some of them may be false. But the important point is that they are capable of being true or false – they are *truth-apt*, to use the standard term – and that whether they are true or false will depend on the way the world really is. So, fundamentally, scientific realism is about the kinds of things scientific theories are, and since theories are part of language (even if what they are about is not), it is to do with our understanding of the language we use when we do science. A *non-realist* view about scientific theories will reject some aspect of the realist's account of how scientific language functions. On one non-realist view, for example, explanations of phenomena in terms of 'ions' is just a useful model by which we can classify those phenomena and predict further phenomena.

Just to make one important clarification before we generalise to other kinds of discourse: the kinds of sentence that realists are interested in are *indicative* sentences, such as 'The Earth orbits the Sun', 'There are an infinite number of prime numbers', 'Stealing is wrong'; the kinds of sentence, that is, that purport to describe things. From now on, we will call such sentences *statements*. Contrast these with non-indicative sentences, such as commands ('Silence!'), wishes ('Oh, to be in England!') or expressions of feeling ('Howl! Howl! Howl!').

Generalising, we will say that *realism about a certain kind of discourse* (scientific, mathematical, moral, etc.) holds the following tenets concerning the statements of that discourse:

(i)   They are *truth-apt*: that is, capable of being true or false;
(ii) They are *irreducible*: that is, they cannot be replaced by sentences which have a different subject-matter without loss of factual content;
(iii) Their purpose is to be *objectively fact-stating*: they are intended as saying something about the world as it is, independently of our beliefs, attitudes or conventions about the subject matter of those statements.

The notion of 'factual content' should be explained. For the realist, the statements in question have factual content in the sense that there are facts which would make them true or false. Those same facts cannot be conveyed by sentences about other things. The fact that an English sentence can be translated into (and so in a sense be replaced by one in) French, German, Greek, Japanese, etc., is quite irrelevant. English sentences about ions may be translated into German, but the German translations will still have the same subject matter, namely ions. In contrast, and to use a different example, if all talk about mental states could be replaced by statements about actual or possible behaviour (as a certain kind of behaviourism asserts), since it is really facts about behaviour which make true statements about mental states, then that *would* be a reduction of mental state talk.

Let us turn to realism about religious discourse. We will struggle to find an all-encompassing definition of 'religious' discourse, so let us focus on the kinds of discourse around which the realism debate has tended to centre. First, we have discourse about God characterised as a transcendent being. That is, at least, a being not constrained or bound by the conditions which constrain our lives, and perhaps more than that, one whose existence and nature are beyond investigation by science. Such discourse might include such statements as 'God created the world'; 'God is the ground of moral value'; 'God loves us and has a plan for the human race', and so on. Then we have discourse about our own nature, purpose and destiny which, though not explicitly referring to God, might nevertheless be closely connected with it. In this category we encounter such sentences as 'We have souls which survive our bodily death'; 'The purpose of life on Earth is to prepare us for Heaven.'

Let's say, then, that we have identified a particular religious discourse composed of statements such as these. Realism about this discourse can be defined by applying the above tenets to religious statements: (i) they are truth-apt; (ii) the religious component is irreducible: they cannot be replaced, without loss of factual content, by non-religious discourse; and (iii) their purpose is to be objectively fact-stating: they are intended as saying something about the world as it is independently of our beliefs, attitudes or conventions concerning religious objects. And, if true, then any religious entities posited by those sentences, such as God, really exist.

Tenets (i)–(iii) all concern the way in which religious statements are to be understood. They imply nothing about whether those sentences are in fact true or false. Suppose the statements in question are about God. The traditional believer will not only take a realist view of them but also take them to be actually *true*. The traditional atheist will similarly take a realist view of them but in addition hold that they are *false*. The traditional agnostic will also be a realist but will neither assent to nor dissent from them. Some writers propose adding a further success condition to the characterisation of realism. Andrew Eshleman, for example, includes the following: 'At least some religious propositions successfully refer to and/or describe a non-natural transcendent entity' (Eshleman (2016): 165). I follow Peter Byrne (2003), however, in adopting a more neutral conception, based on the intended function of the language rather than its success in that function, as I want to emphasise the common ground between traditional believers, atheists and agnostics.

A *non-realist* about religious discourse then, is one who denies one or more of (i)–(iii), and since it is possible to deny just one or two of them, as well as all three, we can define the different varieties of non-realism in terms of which tenets they deny and which, if any, they accept.

I said above that (i)–(iii) concern the way in which religious statements are to be understood. But there is an ambiguity about this which we should banish before proceeding. There are two quite different questions we might ask about statements of a certain kind: (1) How, as a matter of fact, are they understood by those who use them? (2) How *should* they be understood, if they are to play the kind of role we want them to (e.g., to sustain a religious life)? Answers to the first are *descriptive*, describing actual practices and understandings. Answers to the second are *prescriptive*, enjoining us to use and understand the statements in a certain way. In this Element we will mainly be concerned with the prescriptive issue, but at points I will draw attention to the distinction between the two issues.

It will also be helpful, in what follows, to distinguish between the *realist about religious discourse*, which encompasses the theist, atheist and (traditional) agnostic, and the narrower category of the *religious realist*. The latter I will take to be someone who not only takes a realist line with respect to a given religious discourse, but who also bases their active engagement with the religion in question on that realist view. The traditional believer will go one step further: their active engagement with religion involves the attitude of *belief* towards what they take to be expressed by religious discourse. They may even insist that belief is the mark of genuine religious engagement. We will describe the view that belief is the proper attitude towards the content of religious discourse as *doxastic religious realism*, or 'doxasticism' for short (from the Greek δόξα = belief or opinion). This further qualification might seem to be redundant, but an idea which has received increasing attention in recent years is that something less than full belief in the truth of, but still representing a positive response towards religious propositions can be the basis of active religious engagement. This positive attitude might be described as 'commitment' or 'acceptance' (see, e.g., Pojman (1986) and Howard-Snyder (2013)). The resulting view we will call *non-doxastic religious realism*, or 'non-doxasticism' for short. This epistemically more modest view we will encounter again later in the discussion.

1.2 Motivating Realism (1): the Argument from Historical Intention

Why be a realist about religious discourse? One argument is historical. The originators of the discourse intended a realist view of their utterances and writings. We have inherited that discourse, and we simply misuse it if we don't similarly take a realist view. To take a non-religious example, consider the local newspaper. The sane reader of this paper will assume that its contributors intend to give accurate accounts of salient events in the locality: elections to the Parish Council, closure of the public library, proposals to build a bypass, the results of sporting fixtures, notices of forthcoming village galas and 'fun days', and dances at the village hall with Jim on the organ. Heavily figurative language and cynical attempts to manipulate the reading public by propaganda and wild fantasy will be at a minimum. The texts of the various articles were clearly written in a realist spirit, and to interpret them in any other way would defeat their purpose of providing useful and modestly interesting information.

The case of religious documents is perhaps not quite so straightforward. This covers sacred texts, reflections on those texts, statements of doctrine, liturgical texts and so on. These constitute a varied array, and discerning the intentions of the people that wrote them is not always an easy task. Different texts may perform different functions. Some, such as liturgical texts, are plainly instructions and not intended as making assertions. But among the documents that appear to describe things as being a certain way, some look as if they were simply telling fictional stories with a moral point: the parables of Jesus, for example. Nevertheless, for at least some religions, we can identify what look like statements of core doctrine, such as the Thirty-Nine Articles of Religion in the Book of Common Prayer. Some are the outcome of deliberations of various councils set up precisely to codify and regularise doctrine, and explicitly set aside certain heretical variants that had become rife. Looking at the tone of such statements – for example, the threat of excommunication aimed at those who persist in their heretical beliefs – it is a pretty inescapable conclusion that these statements of doctrine were intended to convey truths in as explicit and unambiguous form as possible. Why else would there be dire warnings of the consequences of denying them? Why, indeed, would those warnings be put into dramatic and indeed, in some cases, violent effect? Anything other than a realist interpretation would obscure their true purpose.

· If we suppose that the originators of these core religious statements, the ones taken to be definitive of the religion in question, had access to the truth – perhaps they were divinely inspired – then we have a further reason to interpret them realistically: they provide us with access to the truth, too. Atheists will deny this, and agnostics will remain neutral, but they will still see the force of the argument from historical intention, as it allows them to state their own views on whether or not these texts provide access to the truth.

Still, it might be argued, even if we accept a realist interpretation of such statements in their original context, it remains an open question whether the continued use of this kind of discourse should similarly be given a realist gloss. Why should we not reinterpret the discourse, provide it with an alternative meaning, in such a way as to meet contemporary needs? Recall the distinction between, on the one hand, a *descriptive* account of the way in which a discourse has in fact been used in a particular age and society, and, on the other, a *prescriptive* account of how the discourse should be used in our current context. Perhaps, realistically construed, these religious writings are no longer texts for our times. But reconstrued, they may yet have an important function – a moral and spiritual function – to serve. As we shall see, that is precisely the kind of move non-realists will appeal to.

In reply, the realist may point to the importance of continuity with the past. One of the benefits of a religion is the contribution it makes to social cohesiveness. Membership in a society involves practices and traditions based on consciousness of a shared past. In the case of religion, the realist may argue, what remains from the past is not mere forms of words and ritualised behaviour (attending church, kneeling, singing, fasting and so on), but a grasp of how those forms of words are to be understood and the way in which they inform that behaviour. To put it bluntly: our forebears were realists about religion; we have inherited their religious culture, so we too should be realists. Put like that, the argument looks a bit too quick, but the realist can reinforce it with another.

1.3 Motivating Realism (2): the Argument from the Efficacy of Belief

Defenders of religion point to its benefits: it helps us lead better lives. Immersion in a religion will (it is often suggested) bring about a moral transformation; it helps us to get in focus what really matters in life; and it reorients us to the world in such a way that we feel less alienated, and so happier. What religion is recommended on the basis that it will turn us into miserable moral pygmies?

But this potential transformation, argues the religious realist, requires the right attitude. As the doxastic religious realist would put it, only if we *believe* the core assertions of religion will we see clearly how we ought to be, what our purpose is, and what our destinies are. A view of religion as just so much imagery and arbitrary ritual will be quite impotent. (The non-doxasticist will say something very similar but will substitute their favoured attitude for 'believe'.)

Take as an example the assertion 'God is love.' The power of this statement, understood as the realist understands it, can hardly be overestimated. If the creator of all things embodies the ideal of love, then the world is not fundamentally either indifferent or hostile, for we are loved by this being, and there are the strongest possible grounds for hope that, in some sense, good will prevail. If, on the other hand, the statement is merely symbolic of our own ideals, no such inferences can be made. Further, the realist understanding of 'God is love' has practical implications for the way we should conduct our lives in that it places love among the things of paramount importance. We might think this true quite independently of any religious underpinning, but the religious realist story (if true) gives it an absolute authority it would otherwise lack.

Take another example: 'Our souls are immortal.' If this is literally true, then we do not have to fear death, or at least should not be dismayed by the prospect of it, since it is no more than the end of a certain phase of our existence. And it puts our bodily lives in the context of something much wider so that life on Earth may be seen simply as a preparation for that further, perhaps purer, existence. Not that all this is strictly implied by the bare statement 'our souls are immortal', but it can be part of an elaboration of a view of death that cannot but change the way we view our lives and, perhaps, live them.

In sum, to take religious discourse more or less at face value *and* to believe it true is to enjoy benefits not available to non-believers. Putting this argument for realism together with the previous argument from historical intention we have the following line of thought. We might value our religious inheritance simply as an interesting and instructive historical artefact, viewing it as we might view the remains of a Viking settlement, a Roman mosaic or a medieval text: something to be preserved, aesthetically appreciated and studied for what it might tell us of a past civilisation. If this is how we view it (and no doubt many visitors to cathedrals approach them in just this spirit), then we are under no obligation to treat that religious inheritance in the same way as the people whose religion it was, just as our view of historical remains will not be that of the people whose villages, homes, possessions or legal texts they were. But if we want actively to engage in that religious inheritance, to make it ours as those past peoples made it theirs, then we cannot divorce the outward forms of that religion from the fundamental beliefs animating them. That our forebears intended their core religious discourse in a realist sense is a reason for us, who value our inheritance as a living thing, to use it in the same way. Otherwise, we are merely playacting, like the members of a historical re-enactment society.

These considerations, note, do not provide an argument for religious truth but rather for the thesis that a successful religion must be based on *belief* in its truth.

Having sketched some considerations in favour of realism, we now turn to a series of challenges.

1.4 Challenging Realism

A challenge to religious belief is not invariably – in fact, perhaps it is relatively rarely – posed as a challenge specifically to the realist outlook. There have been plenty of challenges to religious belief. Here is just a selection: the arguments for the existence of God are either fallacious or based on demonstratively false premises; the existence of intense and gratuitous suffering is conclusive proof against an all-powerful, all-knowing and all-loving being; religious doctrines are, if not irredeemably obscure, at best pre-scientific hypotheses about natural phenomena which have long been superseded by wholly natural explanations; religion represents not social progress but social immaturity, and correspondingly, religious belief is not a source of moral growth but rather of moral and emotional infantilism. (Representative, if somewhat polemical, defences of these objections can be found in Dawkins (2006) and Hitchens (2007).) But all these objections to religion are based on a realist assumption: they assume that a realist understanding of religious discourse is the appropriate one. Precisely because of this, however, non-realists may see in these objections reasons to favour a view of religion which avoids these problems precisely by rejecting the assumption on which they are based, and thus as paving the way for an acceptance of religion on a radically different basis.

So let us recast these objections in a slightly more considered way, making it clear whether the challenge they pose is to a wider view, namely realism about religious discourse, or to a more narrowly defined one, namely religious realism, or more narrowly still, namely doxastic religious realism. In what follows, I will assume that we are focusing here specifically on theistic religion.

First, there is the *problem of warrant*. If the sentences of religious discourse make assertions about the world, what is the warrant for thinking them true? There are the traditional arguments for the existence of God, and these have been reworked in quite sophisticated ways in modern times. But they are, to say the least, controversial. And, what is perhaps more to the point, religious believers often resist the idea that their belief should depend on the success of these arguments. Their faith was not the outcome of careful analysis of those arguments, and it is unshaken by attempts to demonstrate that they fail. Nor are they prepared to cite other evidence which unambiguously points to the existence of a transcendent being. Shouldn't this be rather puzzling? In other contexts, the holding of beliefs without adequate evidential warrant would be regarded as a sign of irrationality. Imagine someone forming a firm belief in some historical or scientific hypothesis – that we gained our ancient technological knowledge from benevolent visiting aliens, for example – without having correspondingly firm evidence to ground that belief: wouldn't they be justly criticised for doing so? So why should the case of religious belief be any different? Is there some other, non-evidential warrant available? Or is the notion of warrant inapplicable here? (For a guide to the various debates connected to the issue of religious warrant, see Forrest (1997).)

One particularly challenging aspect of the problem of warrant is the *problem of religious diversity*: there is not one religion, but many, and where the metaphysical and moral outlook of one religion appears to conflict with that of another, the adherents of the one must take adherents of the other to be mistaken. But how do they know this? C. S. Lewis puts the point well when he recalls in his semi-autobiographical *Surprised by Joy* the attitude of his school teachers on the religious views of ancient cultures:

> The accepted position seemed to be that religions were normally a mere farrago of nonsense, though our own, by a fortunate exception, was exactly true ... the impression I got was that religion in general, though utterly false, was a natural growth, a kind of endemic nonsense into which humanity tended to blunder. In the midst of a thousand such religions stood our own, the thousand and first, labelled True. But on what grounds could I believe in this exception? It obviously was in some general sense the same kind of thing as all the rest. Why was it so differently treated? (Lewis (1955): 55)

The challenge posed by the problem of warrant (and the related problem of religious diversity) is clearly a challenge, not to realists in general, but more specifically to doxasticists, that is, to those realists who base their religious engagement on belief. And for those doxasticists who either deny that such warrant is needed or assert that the warrant in question is of a quite different type from the evidential warrant required for historical or scientific beliefs, the challenge is to explain why religious belief should be so different from other belief systems. As for diversity, the doxastic realist seems to face an uncomfortable dilemma: either there is widespread religious error, or all (or at least most) religions must contain some central core of truth, though that truth must be so general and abstract as to be almost without content. (For an attempt to define a meaningful central core to religious world-views, see Hick (1989).)

Second, there is the well-known *problem of evil, or suffering*: how can the evident fact of suffering, indeed intense suffering from which no adequately compensating good seems to ensue, be reconciled with the existence of God as traditionally conceived: a God who loves us, knows about our suffering, and could have prevented it? (For different versions of this problem, compare Mackie (1982) and Rowe (1990).) A further twist of this particular knife is the problem of *religious* evil (see, e.g., Kodaj (2014)): anti-religious polemic urges that religious commitment has historically been, and indeed continues to be, a source of division, oppression, suffering and even violence. It is a source, in short, not of good, but of evil. Is it not ironic, to put it mildly, that the attempt to understand and get close to a loving God should cause so much hatred?

The target of this challenge is perhaps slightly wider than that of the problem of warrant. It is certainly a challenge to doxasticists: how can they continue to believe in such a God? But it is also something of a challenge to non-doxasticists: how can even an attitude of acceptance or commitment to theistic assertions be sustained in the light of what appears to be strong evidence of the falsity of those assertions? Either there must be some reasonably plausible response to the problem of evil, or there must be an account of how belief/acceptance is sustainable in the absence of such an explanation.

Third, there is the *problem of meaning*. How do the words that characterise religious, and in particular theological, discourse, such as 'God', 'creation', 'grace', 'salvation', and so on, acquire their meanings? It is possible, perhaps, to define them in terms of other terms which have an accessible meaning in non-religious contexts. But critics are often warned not to interpret too literally the terms used to explain theological terms, to bring too many of their ordinary connotations to religious discussion. Perhaps terms such as 'person', as applied to God, have to be used in an extended, perhaps metaphorical, sense. There is nothing immediately contrary to realism in this. There is a difference between a realist approach to religious discourse and a wholly literal approach to it (Coakley (2002): 156–9). Perhaps it is not always possible or appropriate to take the terms in religious statements absolutely at face value. What is crucial to the realist view is that such statements cannot be replaced without loss of factual content by non-religious statements. That is entirely consistent with non-religious terms being imported into religious statements and there used in a special, extended or metaphorical sense. Indeed, just this move may be required to avoid the criticism that these statements are implausible, incoherent, or readily falsifiable. But the further we move from the ordinary meanings of words when using them in a religious context, the more problematic specification of their actual meaning becomes. If, as is sometimes said, God can only be described by means of metaphor, and it is not possible to explain this metaphorical language in terms of the non-metaphorical, then it is hard to see how we could possibly know what we mean when we use theological language. (See White (2010): 183–5; see also discussion of different theories of metaphor in Soskice (1987): Ch. III.)

This directly gives rise to a fourth problem, the *problem of reference*: it is a realist tenet that if religious discourse contains genuinely referring terms, they refer to entities that exist independently of beliefs, attitudes or conventions. As one might put it, one does not need a religion for there to be religious objects. But how do these religious terms succeed in picking out their referents? Do they do so by being what Saul Kripke (1972) called 'descriptive names'? That is, are they equivalent to definite descriptions which are uniquely satisfied by real objects? But if those descriptions do not have determinate content, or are irreducibly metaphorical, then they are not up to the job of picking out anything determinate. Perhaps, however, there is another way of securing reference other than by description: by the right kind of causal relation between the user of the names and some external entity. One might imagine reference being secured through the means of religious experience. 'The object of my thought is whatever *that* is.' But then the worry is that without some disambiguating description, such demonstrative attempts will pick out more than one object.

Both the problem of meaning and the associated problem of reference are challenges to those religious realists who want to resist a too-literal understanding of religious terms. Those who are both realist about, and hostile to (and hostile *because* realist about) religious discourse might prefer to clarify their own position by assigning some fairly definite meanings to religious terms.

Much has been written on these four problems, and especially the first two. It is not my intention, in this very short Element, to discuss realist responses to these challenges. But I do want to consider the extent to which fictionalism avoids them. I also want to mention a fifth challenge to realism, one which has received rather less attention than the other four: the *problem of moral seriousness*. As we saw above, one source of motivation for realism is the thought that only religious realism can deliver a truly religious life, that is, one which fully exploits religion's power to form us as moral beings. Non-realists have tried to turn the tables by arguing that actually it is the *realist* who exhibits a lack of true religious seriousness, because the realist lacks true moral seriousness (see, e.g., Cupitt (1980): 9–10). The charge of moral and emotional infantilism alluded to above is a significant aspect of this challenge.

Here is how the discussion will proceed. In Section 2, we look at non-realist positions which emerged from a historically important and influential version of the problem of warrant, a version which also poses a problem of meaning. In Section 3, we develop one of these non-realist approaches, fictionalism, in more detail, and consider how it deals with central aspects of the religious life such as prayer and moral commitment. Can it avoid the realist's charge that it exhibits a lack of religious seriousness? Or does that charge rebound on the realist? In Section 4, we ask whether fictionalism faces its own version of the problem of evil.

Is realism the natural view? Since such religious expressions as 'God created the world', 'God loves us', 'Death is not final', and 'We will be saved' *look* like assertions, it is natural to treat them as if they *are* assertions. And since they do not point to anything in our immediate experience, it is natural to take them as referring (or as intended to refer) to something beyond that experience. But perhaps appearances can be deceptive.

2 Non-Realism: the Garden of Forking Paths

The object of religion is conduct.

Matthew Arnold, *Literature and Dogma* (1884)

2.1 A Verificationist Prelude

Perhaps the most uncompromising attack on theological language appeared in A. J. Ayer's landmark book *Language, Truth and Logic* (1936). Ayer does not explicitly present it as an attack on realism specifically: it is presented rather as a demonstration that theological statements are meaningless. He does not, indeed, acknowledge the possibility of a non-realist treatment of theological discourse (though, interestingly, he does acknowledge, and indeed defends, a non-realist treatment of moral discourse). But if he is right, then realism about theological discourse is unsustainable. His argument would not, I suspect, find many adherents today, at least in the form in which he put it, but it is most certainly of historical interest, as it led directly to an influential statement and defence of religious non-realism, the components of which we will examine in this section.

In the first chapter Ayer presents a criterion for the meaningfulness of assertions which he calls the 'criterion of verifiability'. In his words:

> We say that a sentence is factually significant to any given person, if, and only if, he knows how to verify the proposition which it purports to express – that is, if he knows what observations would lead him, under certain conditions, to accept the proposition as being true, or reject it as being false. If, on the other hand, the putative proposition is of such a character that the assumption of its truth, or falsehood, is consistent with any assumption whatsoever concerning the nature of his future experience, then, as far as he is concerned, it is, if not a tautology, a mere pseudo-proposition. The sentence expressing it may be emotionally significant to him; but it is not literally significant. (Ayer (1936): 48)

This criterion is the core of a view of meaning known as *verificationism*. Ayer defines 'tautology' as a sentence which 'is true solely in virtue of the meaning of its constituent symbols' (Ayer (1946): 21). Another term for this is 'analytic truth', the criterion for which is that its denial would be self-contradictory. An example of an analytic truth would be 'All vixens are female', which is true by virtue of the fact that 'vixen' just *means* 'female fox.' It is not a hypothesis about the nature of foxes, to be tested by examining each fox in turn. ('Is this a vixen? Yes. Is it female? Yes. Oh, good.') Tautologies may tell us something about language, but they do not tell us anything about how the world is. A 'factually significant sentence', in contrast, is intended as telling us something about the world (though it may turn out to be false). Consider 'There is a blood stain on the library carpet.' This is certainly not true by definition or stipulation, and establishing its truth would require a close study of the carpet in the library. Factual significance is not the only kind of significance, as Ayer concedes. The criterion here is directed specifically at *indicative* sentences, or *statements*, which appear to tell us how things are. It does not apply to commands, wishes or unstructured expressions of feeling such as 'ow!' In a later, and more concise, formulation, Ayer puts the criterion like this: 'a statement is held to be literally meaningful if and only if it is either analytic or empirically verifiable' ((1946): 12), or falsifiable, we might add, following the lines of his earlier definition.

Ayer sees that the verifiability principle should be stated in terms, not of conclusive verification, but rather of *confirmation*. He considers the statement 'all men are mortal' ((1936): 50). This is plainly a meaningful statement, but it can never be conclusively verified, as it is not possible to inspect every man to verify that he is mortal. However, a single observation of a man's being mortal is a confirming instance of the general statement that every man is mortal. And the more confirming instances there are, the more likely the statement is to be true.

An alternative way to state the criterion is that if a statement is a genuinely contentful assertion about the world, then whether it is true or false should have some experiential significance. It should, in other words, make some types of experience more likely than others. If a statement is not only compatible with any possible experience whatsoever, but has no implications for the probability of any possible experience, then it is not really to do with how things are. Scientific hypotheses pass the verifiability criterion because there is some procedure, or set of procedures, which would tend to confirm them. The theory itself should predict observable phenomena, and so make some observational outcomes more likely than others. A hypothesis that could not be confirmed in this way, a hypothesis which fits equally well with any observation at all, would be labelled 'unscientific.' Indeed, it is scientific language that, for the verificationist, sets the standard for determinate meaningfulness.

Theological statements, according to Ayer, fail this test and so are meaningless. But this clearly requires some qualification. 'God created the world' can hardly be put on the same level as the ill-formed 'Ways insofar a joyful under grazing of', or the grammatically well-formed but still nonsensical 'He took his vorpal sword in hand: Long time the manxome foe he sought.' We can at least attempt to link the components of 'God created the world' with concepts acquired from other contexts. But since theological statements do not satisfy the verifiability principle, they lack *factual* meaning: they do not succeed in making an intelligible statement about the world.

Are theological statements unverifiable? One possible response is to say that, although we cannot currently put theological statements and associated ones, such as 'We have immortal souls', to an empirical test, we could (in principle) do so at some point in the future. This is the procedure of what we might call 'posthumous verification' (or as John Hick calls it, 'eschatological verification', Hick (1960): 58f): if we are indeed immortal, and there is a God, then we can expect to be apprised of both of these facts after our bodily deaths. This initially appears straightforward. However, when it comes to providing more details of what this experience would be like, we are somewhat at a loss. What is the nature of life after bodily death? Can we make sense of disembodied experience? Or will we have some alternative kind of body? The impossibility of answering these questions means that we cannot say anything very informative about what experience would be like which would give content to those religious statements.

Another response goes as follows. The tradition of natural theology has produced a number of arguments for the existence of God that are based on observed features of the universe. If the world was designed, then we might expect to see evidence of a designer. Earlier versions of what has become known as the teleological argument pointed to such evidence as the adaptability of organisms to their environment. But the advent of evolutionary theory and Darwin's account of biological adaptation in terms of natural selection considerably weakened the force of that version of the argument. More recently, natural theologians have pointed to the so-called 'fine-tuning' of the universe. If any of the so called 'fundamental constants' of physics had had a slightly different value, life could not have developed. Given that there is no reason within physics we could appeal to in order to explain why the constants have the values they do, it seems to follow that the emergence of life was vanishingly improbable. Unless, that is, we appeal to an all-powerful creator who fixed those values with the ultimate aim of allowing human life to develop. (For discussion of the 'fine tuning' argument and a non-religious alternative explanation of the data, see Leslie (1989).)

Ayer concedes that putative evidence has been put forward for the existence of God. His surprising response to this takes us further into the verificationist conception of meaning:

> It is sometimes claimed, indeed, that the existence of a certain sort of regularity in nature constitutes sufficient evidence for the existence of a god. But if the sentence 'God exists' entails no more than that certain types of phenomena occur in certain sequences, then to assert the existence of a god

will be simply equivalent to asserting that there is the requisite regularity in nature; and no religious man would admit that this was all he intended to assert in asserting the existence of a god. (Ayer (1936): 152)

That argument certainly goes rather fast! What, we might wonder, is the connection between the first two sentences of this passage? Granted that the regularity of the universe is evidence of the truth of 'God exists', why would it follow that 'God exists' just *means* that the universe exhibits regularities? As Michael Scott (2017) puts it, the argument seems to involve a sleight of hand (see also Scott (2013): 45). What is in play here is a stronger assumption about meaning than the earlier principle of verifiability, the assumption, namely that the truth of A can only be evidence for the truth of B if A is either part or the whole of the meaning of B. But, in a later response to critics, Ayer explicitly disavows this. To use his example: that there is blood on my coat is evidence that I have committed a murder; it does not follow that 'there is blood on my coat' is part of the *meaning* of 'I have committed a murder' (Ayer (1946): 19). However, he goes on to say that the meaning of an assertion about the world is given by a core set of observation statements, the truth of which we would insist on if the assertion in question is to be taken as true. And this core group of statements point to circumstances that we take as confirming the assertion in question, as providing evidence for its truth. Now perhaps 'the universe exhibits regularities' is the kind of thing whose truth we would insist on if 'God exists' is to be taken as true. In which case, it must be part of the meaning of 'God exists'.

This stronger assumption about meaning is highly controversial. And it has interesting consequences for the understanding of the kinds of statement that were supposed to provide the paradigm of meaningful (because verifiable) statements, namely scientific statements – a point we take up below. Fortunately, we are not in the business here of defending verificationism. The point of introducing it is to show how a certain – at one time, very influential – view of meaning led to forms of religious non-realism. And, whatever controversial route was taken to get to them, they are worth discussing in their own right, as we shall now do.

2.2 Religion as Moral Commitment

In 'An Empiricist's View of the Nature of Religious Belief' (1955), Richard Braithwaite explores the consequences of a (suitably modified) verificationist principle of meaning for religious discourse. He begins by quoting the physicist Arthur Eddington: 'The meaning of a scientific statement is to be ascertained by the steps which would be taken to verify it' (Eddington 1939: 189). Braithwaite is happy to endorse this as a principle of scientific meaning, but can it be extended to religious statements? He considers, and dismisses, three possibilities concerning religious statements: (1) that they can be verified by direct observation, in the same kind of way as we might verify 'There is a hedgehog in the garden shed'; (2) that they can be verified in the same way as the theoretical statements of science, such as 'this sample of radium is emitting alpha particles'; (3) that they do not need empirical verification because they are like the statements of logic and mathematics, and so do not imply the existence of any object in the world. (They are 'analytic', in the sense introduced in the previous section.) (1) and (3) are plainly not appropriate accounts of religious statements. Even devout believers do not take God to be a directly observable object like a tree, and the properties attributed to God, such as his being personal, or all-powerful, or all-knowing, are not directly observable either. Believers might, indeed, take the statement 'God exists' to be necessary, but not, surely, in the same sense as '2 + 2 = 4' is necessary. The believer is not merely making a point about relations between concepts but (at least, this is how the realist would view it) about what there is in the world.

So what of the remaining possibility? Could statements about God be compared to statements about the theoretical (and so not directly observable) entities of science, such as alpha particles? Here Brathwaite poses a challenge: would those who are committed to religious statements abandon them in the light of any empirical discovery? Or would the newly discovered facts invariably be reconciled with those religious statements, perhaps by appeal to some further hypothesis? Suppose, for example, that discoveries were made which suggested that all life would be extinct within ten years, or that the wicked tended to prosper over the good, or that religious experiences were the product of some brain malfunction, or that some holy text was in fact manufactured by a fraudster, or a hundred other unsettling revelations. Would any of those impinge in the slightest on one's commitment to the religious statements in question? If the answer to this is 'no', then there is no empirical content to these statements. As Braithwaite puts it:

> Philosophers of religion who wish to make empirical facts relevant to the meaning of religious statements but at the same time desire to hold on to those statements whatever the empirical facts may be are indulging, I believe, in a sort of *doublethink* attitude: they want to hold that religious statements both are about the actual world (i.e. are empirical statements) and also are not refutable in any possible world, the characteristic of statements which are logically necessary. (Braithwaite (1955): 76)

One might expect at this point that Braithwaite, like Ayer, would conclude that religious statements are meaningless, but he does not. Recognising that, for certain kinds of sentence, meaning is not always determined by verification procedures, he proposes an extension of the verificationist principle: that the meaning of a sentence is given by the way in which that sentence is used. Empirical sentences are used to make assertions which are (directly or indirectly) confirmable or disconfirmable by experience. But moral discourse, for example, is not like this. The statement 'one should never break a promise' is not something that can be confirmed by any number of instances of people keeping their promises, nor disconfirmable by any instance of someone breaking their promise. So, according to verificationism, it is not stating a fact. What else might it be doing? One possibility is that it expresses a feeling of approval towards the keeping of promises and disapproval towards the breaking of promises. This is the view of moral statements defended by Ayer: they are expressive of feelings of approval or disapproval for certain actions (Ayer (1936): 107f). But Braithwaite rejects this account on the grounds that emotions are not fundamental to moral utterances. Such utterances may, indeed, be accompanied by such feelings, but their central purpose is to express intentions to pursue a certain course of action: to intend to keep promises, for example. And indeed, there is a greater sense of anomaly in the case of someone who insists that promise-breaking is wrong and yet who exhibits no disposition to keep their promises than in the case of someone who acts according to their moral precepts in a completely dispassionate way and is unmoved by others' failure to act in accordance with them. The meaning of a moral statement, then, is given by the relevant *intention to act* which it is used to express. (Braithwaite talks of moral *assertions*, but it seems best to avoid the word when truth or falsity is not at issue.)

Religious discourse, suggests Braithwaite, can be assimilated to moral discourse: it too is expressive of commitments to a certain course of action:

> The view which I put forward for your consideration is that the intention of a Christian to follow a Christian way of life is not only the criterion for the sincerity of his belief in the assertions of Christianity; it is the criterion for the meaningfulness of his assertions. (Braithwaite (1955): 80)

We can, at least in principle, apply this general template to other religions. But there is an immediate objection, as Braithwaite realises. For whereas with moral sentences, such as 'eating people is wrong', it is immediately apparent what course of action is being committed to (viz., refraining from eating people), religious statements do not make explicit which commitment to action is being expressed. They do not wear their meanings on their sleeves, so to speak. Braithwaite's solution is to suggest that it is the body of related religious sentences *as a whole* that is given meaning by the relevant commitments, rather than individual sentences taken in isolation. This parallels the meaning of scientific statements: it is only in conjunction with other, related, scientific statements that their observational consequences can be derived and tested against experience.

This provides an interesting view of religious conversion. Instead of seeing this as a case of someone's coming to appreciate the truth of some set of religious assertions, we can view it as their deciding to enter into a particularly rigorous set of moral and behavioural commitments.

But if religious discourse is to be assimilated to moral discourse in this way, what is the difference between them? For surely, we want to say there is some difference. A moral person is not necessarily a religious person. Here, Braithwaite points to two features that characterise religion, but not morality in general. One is that the undertaking that the religious person enters into is not simply a matter of external behaviour (giving to the poor, putting others' needs before one's own), but relates also to the internal life – to love one's neighbour as oneself, for example. It involves a change in one's emotional attitude. Braithwaite's view, as he points out, could be seen to be prefigured in Matthew Arnold's dictum that religion is 'morality touched by emotion' (Arnold (1884): 16).

The second aspect of religion that is not typically characteristic of morality in general is the narratives, stories, and parables that constitute part of the cultural inheritances of a religion, and which helps to define the religious community in question. Consider, for example, the Christian narrative of creation, the Fall and redemption through the sacrifice of God's Son upon the cross, the parables of Jesus and the story of his life. The differences between religions, indeed, may be more to do with the differences between their narratives, and the inherited examples of appropriate behaviour than the abstract moral principles.

What Braithwaite is recommending is clearly a non-realist account of religious discourse. Consider again the various components of realism set out in the previous chapter. On Braithwaite's proposal (as discussed so far), none of these would appear to apply. Sentences expressing practical commitments (I undertake to do such-and-such) are not capable of being true or false. If the meaning of religious sentences (or at least, a set of related religious sentences) is wholly given by their use in expressing such commitments, then replacement by a non-religious language without loss of factual content *is* possible. His conception of religious discourse is an *expressivist* one: religious sentences express *non-cognitive* attitudes. A 'cognitive attitude' is one that represents the world as being a certain way, and is capable of corresponding, or not corresponding, to the facts. Belief is an example of a cognitive attitude. A non-cognitive attitude, in contrast, is one which cannot appropriately be evaluated as corresponding or not corresponding to the facts. Disgust is an example of a non-cognitive attitude. (A non-cognitive attitude might well accompany a cognitive one: you might feel disgust precisely because you believe that the hotel room has not been cleaned in a decade.) There is more than one kind of expressivism, however. As we have seen, he rejects one expressivist position: the view that what is expressed is an emotion. We might call this rejected view *emotive expressivism*. Since the kind of states Braithwaite focuses on – intentions, commitments – are sometimes called (and are called by him) 'conative' states, we might dub his position *conative expressivism*.

What objections might be raised against Braithwaite's conative expressivism? First, it could be accused of misrepresenting the intentions of most, if not quite all, religious communities (and in particular the Christian believers that Braithwaite has most clearly in focus). Since he is operating with a rather uncompromising principle of meaningfulness, Braithwaite is offering, in the terms introduced in the previous section, a descriptive account of religious language. But, as a number of commentators (such as Richard Swinburne (1977): 86–7) have pointed out, although Christian (and other) believers may express behavioural commitments when they utter religious statements, it is very implausible to suggest that this is *all* they mean: many of them also intend to make an assertion about what is in fact the case. The point should be conceded, but that is not the end of the matter, since Braithwaite's view can still be presented as a prescriptive account of religious discourse.

Whether descriptive or prescriptive, Braithwaite's expressivism faces three further objections. The first is what we might call the *problem of meaning collapse*. If any two statements made within a religious tradition – even those that appear to be in tension – express the same behavioural commitments (to live for others, for instance), then on the expressivist view they will mean the same thing. It is an unappealing consequence of Braithwaite's appeal to the holism of religious meaning (it is the body of religious statements taken in its entirety that expresses the set of behavioural commitments in question) that it will be impossible to assign individual meanings to different statements. And associating different statements with different religious stories will not help, since it seems in principle possible to associate the same religious sentences with different religious stories, or different statements with the same story, or with no story at all (Scott (2013): 52–3).

A second, related, objection is the *problem of meaning relativity*. The same religious statement, such as 'Mary is the mother of God', may suggest different forms of commitment from one individual to another: one to pray to Mary as the intermediary between God and humankind, another to try to imitate Mary's virtuous behaviour. Within an expressivist scheme, however, this would entail that the meaning of a statement will be relative to the individuals using them: there is no fixed meaning (Scott (2013): 51–2).

A final objection is this: if asked *why* they want to commit to a particular course of action, what rationalises their decision, religious people are likely to say such things as 'Because God commands it', 'Because a loving God would want us to behave in this way', or 'Because God forgives us', or 'Because that is what scripture teaches.' These, at least at first sight, provide *reasons* for a certain course of action. But for them to play this role, these utterances have to be treated as assertions, and this is precisely what Braithwaite's expressivist denies that they are. If 'God loves us' is, taken in conjunction with other similar expressions, expressive of an intention to lead (e.g.) a Christian life, it cannot provide any reason for living that life. Intentions do not rationalise themselves. Braithwaite has an answer to this objection, which will also help us with the others; but before considering it, let us explore another non-realist view which verificationism might motivate.

2.3 Religion as Experience

Recall the stronger strain of verificationism which holds that the meaning of an assertion is given by the method by which we would verify it in experience. It follows from this that, as Ayer puts it, all factually meaningful expressions consist of (perhaps encoded forms of) observation statements. Although scientific statements were taken by verificationists to be among the paradigm cases of meaningful statements, the result is a controversial view of the theoretical statements employed in science, a view known as *positivism*.

Consider the statement 'The temperature of this liquid is 60 degrees Celsius.' According to the positivist, this is equivalent to a disjunctive set of observation statements, each of which refers to some observable effect. That might be the reading on a mercury thermometer, or the movement of a bimetallic strip, or the colour change of some heat-sensitive material. A similar analysis would be given of a more deeply theoretical statement, such as 'An alpha particle has just been emitted.' This, again, the positivist would treat as equivalent to a set of observation statements which would be taken to confirm the presence of an alpha particle: a visible track in a cloud chamber, the clicking of a Geiger counter, or a photographic trace.

Positivism, in seeking to reduce theoretical statements to observation statements, rests on the assumption that there are such things as pure observation statements – statements which contain no theoretical terms requiring further reduction. The difficulty, however, is that there appear to be no such statements, or, if there are, they will be of no help in reducing the theoretical language.

Consider the observation statements appealed to above in reducing the theoretical statement 'An alpha particle has just been emitted.' To make sense of such expressions as 'cloud chamber' and 'Geiger counter', we have to understand the function of these devices, which itself requires appeal to theory. But a mere description of the appearance of such devices in terms of such things as shape, size and colour will not intimate their function, and so be quite useless in helping us understand, in observational terms, the content of 'an alpha particle has just been emitted.' At least some theoretical content seems to be ineliminable (Newton-Smith (1981): Ch. II).

Even if scientific positivism is in difficulties, however, there may still be a viable religious counterpart. This would hold that the meaning of religious statements is to be cashed out in terms of the experiences which would ordinarily be taken (or at least, taken by the realist) to verify religious beliefs. As for realism, what we might call *religious positivism* allows that religious statements are capable of being true or false. What makes positivism a non-realist position is its rejection of one or more of the other components of realism. Which components? Take the second: religious statements are not reducible to non-religious sentences. Just as scientific positivism seeks to reduce theoretical statements to non-theoretical, purely observational statements, so religious positivism seeks to reduce religious statements to non-religious, purely experiential discourse. And this entails the rejection of the third component of realism: what religious statements are really about (experiences) is not independent of our ways of representing things. But what kind of experiences are such that they would ordinarily be taken to verify religious beliefs and yet have no overt religious content? One answer might be: an awareness of moral obligations. To play any kind of role in a religious life, we cannot here be thinking of an awareness of the obligation to turn the lights out before leaving the office, or of making occasional modest contributions to charity. The sense of moral obligation must be suitably intense and all-encompassing: a sense that one needs to lead a completely different life, as Saul felt on the road to Damascus (Acts 9: 3–9).

Promising though religious positivism might initially seem as a non-realist rival to Braithwaite's proposal, it suffers from analogous difficulties to those facing its scientific counterpart. Just as we cannot eliminate all theoretical content from observation statements if they are to convey adequately the meaning of theoretical statements, so we seem unable to eliminate all religious content from religious statements. If we ask 'what kinds of experiences would ordinarily be taken to confirm religious statements?', the obvious candidates for this role would be *religious* experiences: intimations of a deity, of oneness with the universe, of all-encompassing love, and so on. We cannot wholly reduce the religious component of these experiences without distorting their nature. For what makes them *religious* experiences, what defines their distinctive character, is precisely what they appear to intimate about reality: that there is a God, that the universe is fundamentally benign, that we are the object of infinite love, and so on. The religious content of these experiences – that is, what they appear to be about or directed towards – is what makes them the experiences they are. If we stripped out that content, to focus just on their moral content, or the kinds of emotion and feeling they involve, with no mention of their apparent object, we could not capture what in fact it was like to have those experiences. And what convinced Saul on the road to Damascus that he needed to completely reorient his life was the sense that he was receiving a divine message.

So could the positivist propose that, e.g., a statement purporting to be about a deity is in fact about experiences which are *as of* being appeared to by, or otherwise in contact with, a deity? Not without embarking on a circle of definition. For we cannot understand what it is for an experience to be as of a deity without understanding what is conveyed by 'deity' (and similarly for any other religious term), and if the meaning of 'deity' is to be understood in terms of experience as of a deity, then we have no hope of understanding this – or indeed any other – kind of religious statement.

2.4 Religion as Fiction

So, having briefly explored an alternative to conative expressivism, let us return to the discussion as we left it in Section 2.2, and to one of the challenges posed by the realist: part of the role of appealing to the truth of religious statements, says the realist, is to provide reasons for undertaking moral commitments. That God loves us is a reason for undertaking to love one's neighbour. But if religious statements are nothing more than expressions of moral commitment, they cannot play this role. One cannot make moral commitments appear reasonable by appealing to those same moral commitments!

Braithwaite does not tackle this challenge head on, but what he says about the role of religious stories offers an answer. He concedes that identifying religious statements with expression of moral commitments does not suffice to differentiate one religion from another. What does so, he suggests, are the differences between the various stories that accompany those traditions: there are Christian stories, Buddhist stories, Hindu stories, and so on. It is these stories that play a crucial role in motivating moral commitment and behaviour. If the stories are not believed – and many of them are clearly presented simply as stories, and so not intended to be taken as literal truth – they cannot be presented as reasons for action in the way that what is believed to be the case can. But they can nevertheless have a causal effect on us. Braithwaite explains this in the following terms:

> How is entertaining the story related to resolving to pursue a certain way of life? My answer is that the relation is a psychological and causal one. It is an empirical psychological fact that many people find it easier to resolve upon and to carry through a course of action which is contrary to their natural inclinations if this policy is associated in their mind with certain stories. And in many people the psychological link is not appreciably weakened by the fact that the story associated with the behaviour policy is not believed ... it is completely untrue, as a matter of psychological fact, to think that the only intellectual considerations which affect action are beliefs: it is all the thoughts of a man that determine his behaviour; and these include his phantasies, imaginations, ideas of what he would wish to be and do, as well as the propositions which he believes to be true. (Braithwaite (1955): 86–7)

This suggests another non-realist line – a *fictionalist* one. According to this view, religious statements are propositional, and so evaluable as true or false. But they are only true *within a fiction* – the Christian fiction, or Buddhist fiction, and so on. Insofar as they are fact-stating, they are only *fictional fact*-stating, and so not answerable to a reality which is independent of our beliefs, attitudes or conventions.

There are, then, both expressivist and fictionalist elements in Braithwaite's account of religious discourse. Are they compatible? At one point, he talks as if these two views capture all religious statements: 'To assert the whole set of assertions of the Christian religion is both to tell the Christian doctrinal story and to confess allegiance to the Christian way of life.' (85) This is a perfectly consistent suggestion, by itself. But recall that his original account of the *meaning* of religious statements was in terms of their not being propositional, or fact-stating, but rather expressive of moral commitment. They cannot be *both* propositional (though fictional) *and* non-propositional (because expressive only of non-cognitive attitudes). One way of resolving the tension here is to distinguish the doctrinal statements from the more obviously fictional elements, and to give an expressivist, rather than fictionalist, reading of the former. After all, it is precisely the problems in verifying doctrinal statements (the universe was created by God, God is three persons in one, etc.) that motivated the expressivist reading. In contrast, the stories whose point is to help a religion's adherents live the right kind of life may involve in principle verifiable states of affairs. However, a consideration which militates against a sharp distinction between doctrinal statements and stories in terms of an account of their meaning is that the stories themselves may allude to doctrinal matters: creation, incarnation, resurrection, and so on. The removal of any theoretical elements from the stories may well risk distorting our engagement with them. And indeed Braithwaite's phrase 'to tell the Christian doctrinal story' suggests he is not drawing a firm distinction between doctrinal elements and, say, parables. Perhaps, construed fictionally, doctrinal statements need not be interpreted as something which, if literally true, would be beyond verification. And if the fictionalist manoeuvre is sufficient to avoid verificationist objections, then rather than offering an expressivist account of the meaning of doctrinal statements, Braithwaite might have been best adopting a uniform fictionalist treatment of all religious statements. It is immersion in the religious fiction of our choosing that is the cause (and perhaps more than just the cause) of our subsequently coming to undertake certain moral commitments. Here the possibility of a temporal gap between engaging with the discourse and coming to make the commitments is important. We might engage with the discourse and practices of a religion initially in an experimental spirit. We are not, perhaps, yet ready to undertake the commitments characteristic of full engagement with the religion. But as our involvement with the discourse becomes deeper, so we might find ourselves ready to change the course of our practical lives. However, if that discourse was already understood to be expressive of those commitments, this gap would not make sense. To engage in the discourse would *already* be to make those commitments.

Once the commitment to action is made, however, there is no objection to our taking the use of religious language by the fictionalist to be in part expressive of moral commitment. We do not have to insist that a statement is either wholly descriptive or wholly expressive of intention. A statement can have more than one function. If I say to you 'I do like your hat: it's awfully jolly', I not only state a fact about my preferences; I also express a feeling; I commit to not abusing your hat in the next breath; and I perhaps also intend my remark to have the effect of establishing a rapport between us.

The fictionalist element in Braithwaite's account also provides a means of avoiding the problem of meaning collapse and meaning relativity: different religious statements have different meanings within the religious fiction, and these provide a core common meaning to a given statement, despite its being used, among other things, to express different commitments.

And so we have arrived at a fictionalist conception of religion. But can fictionalism provide an adequate grounding for characteristic and central aspects of a religious life? That is the subject of the next section.

3 Fictionalism and the Religious Life

I find it necessary to distinguish clearly several questions: – 1. How far has Christianity been indispensable or beneficial to the progress of mankind up to the point now reached? 2. How far does it seem beneficial or indispensable at the present stage, or likely to be so in the future?

3. Is it true?

I am not myself disposed to connect 1 or 2 closely with 3.

Henry Sidgwick, letter to J. R. Mozley, 30th July 1881

3.1 Fiction, Pretence and Fictionalisms

Our discussion of Braithwaite provided no more than a sketch of religious fictionalism. We will now try to make it a little more precise before going on to consider whether fictionalism can provide an adequate basis for a religious life.

Let's start with the case of overt fiction. In discussing a novel such as *Great Expectations*, for instance, we want to be able to say things like 'Pip visits Miss Haversham', 'Pip is initially unaware of the source of his good fortune', 'Pip is embarrassed by Joe Gargery's deference to him', and so on, without eliciting the tiresome objection that no such figures actually exist, and that what we are saying is in consequence either contentless or false. What we need, then, is an account of what makes it appropriate to assert such statements. As a first step, we can appeal to the idea that, e.g., 'Pip visits Miss Haversham' is shorthand for the (demonstrably true) 'According to the fiction *Great Expectations,* it is true that Pip goes to see Miss Haversham.' And similarly for any other statement we might make about what is going on in the fiction. The prefix 'According to the fiction (name of fiction) ... ' then insulates what we want to assert from falsification by actual fact. Of course, we need to know what it is for something to be true according to the fiction, and for this we will need a theory of fictional truth. The simplest account, though an unsatisfactory one, identifies what is true with what is explicitly stated on the pages of the novel, or in the words uttered on stage, or by the distribution of lines and colour in the painting, and so forth. The reason that this is unsatisfactory is that some fictional truths are tacit: they aren't explicitly stated, but can reasonably be inferred. An adequate account of fictional truth will have to explain why these unstated fictional truths are nevertheless true. Such an account may appeal to the author's intentions, or what it is reasonable to infer about the author's intentions and beliefs given the author's context, or some variant of these. (For discussion of various approaches to truth in fiction, see Currie (1990).)

There is another class of statement about fiction, however, that may need a rather different treatment, namely *critical* statements. Examples of this would be: 'Joe Gargery represents Dickens's view of the nobility of the humble labourer'; 'Joe Gargery is a less plausible character than Magwitch.' Here, the fictional status of the characters is recognised, and so such assertions would not contain an implicit 'According to the fiction' prefix. It is certainly *not* part of the world of the novel that Joe is a less plausible character than Magwitch! Nor does Dickens make an appearance. For our present purposes, however, critical statements about fiction will be less germane than statements we take to be true *in* the fiction.

Another context in which a statement about fictional characters and events should not, arguably, be supposed to be qualified by an implicit 'according to the fiction' is where such a statement is part of a game of make-believe. Suppose we are narrating the story of *Great Expectations* as part of a performance version of the novel ('And now Pip enters the familiar house, wondering if he will see Estelle.'). Here it is not at all plausible to suggest that we are implicitly asserting 'And now, according to the fiction *Great Expectations*, Pip enters the familiar house.' Making that explicit would certainly ruin the atmosphere of the performance. So how should we understand this kind of statement?

A natural view of what we might call the 'speech act' we perform in saying 'Pip visits Miss Haversham' is that the act is not one of assertion, but rather one of pretence: we do not *actually* assert, but only *pretend* to assert, that Pip visits Miss Haversham. And this is another way in which what we say is insulated from falsification by the external world: pretending to assert is not something that is answerable to the world. There is a sense, though, in which it is answerable to the content of the fiction. For some pretend assertions will be more appropriate in the context of engaging with the fiction than others. It would not be appropriate, in a performance of *Great Expectations*, to say (and thereby pretend to assert) 'And so, as the Battle of Hastings rages, Pip enters the familiar house.' The Battle of Hastings is no part of the fiction. There is a systematic relationship, then, between what is true in, or according to, the fiction, and what it is appropriate to pretend when engaged in that fiction. It is not true in *Great Expectations* that aliens land, and it would not be appropriate, in immersing oneself in the fiction, to pretend that they do.

How much of this can and should be exploited by the fictionalist? It goes without saying that fictionalism is an appropriate view of fiction. Fiction is fictional, after all! But fictionalist approaches have been proposed for a variety of discourses: there is, for example, fictionalism about scientific theories, fictionalism about numbers, fictionalism about possible worlds, and fictionalism about moral values. (See, respectively, van Fraassen (1980), Field (1980), Rosen (1990) and Joyce (2005).) What these have in common is the idea that the attitude that is appropriate in using the discourse, or for engaging in the activity associated with that discourse, is not *truth-normed*. Consider, by way of contrast, an attitude such as belief. You believe, say, that the Moon is not an independent source of light, but only reflects light from the Sun. If it had turned out that this was false, that the Moon was in fact a translucent object with a light source at its centre, and you were apprised of this, then rationality would have dictated that you abandon that belief. Belief is answerable to the world. That is what is meant by saying that belief is 'truth-normed'. Not all attitudes, however, are truth-normed. As we have just seen, pretence is not truth-normed. Pretending that *p* is perfectly acceptable when *p* is known to be false (in fact, such a situation captures much of pretence: let's pretend we're birds, trees, robots, wizards, etc.). Entertaining a thought is also not truth-normed. You may not know whether or not there is extra-terrestrial intelligent life, you may even be inclined to believe that there isn't, but that does not stop you from entertaining the idea, for the purposes, say, of working out its consequences. And entertaining a thought can be quite detached: no pretence need be involved. However, simply entertaining thoughts about a particular subject matter does not automatically make one a fictionalist about that subject. As Mark Eli Kalderon puts it:

> The distinctive commitment of fictionalism is that acceptance in a given domain of inquiry need not be truth-normed, and that acceptance of a sentence from the associated region of discourse need not involve belief in its content. (Kalderon (2005): 2)

Kalderon distinguishes between tentative and full acceptance. The example above of entertaining the notion of extra-terrestrial life in order to work out its consequences would be an example of tentative acceptance. This attitude is perfectly compatible with (indeed may be part of) an attempt to investigate whether there is any truth in the idea. Full acceptance, in contrast, 'ends inquiry', as Kalderon puts it. There is no further felt need to investigate whether one's acceptance is tracking the truth. The definition above is intended to apply only to full acceptance. Bas van Fraassen's (1980) 'constructive empiricism' about scientific theories thus counts, on this definition, as fictionalist. For van Fraassen, although scientific theories are true or false by virtue of features of a mind-independent world, science does not aim at truth but rather what he calls 'empirical adequacy': the capacity of theories to fit with, and to predict, observable phenomena ((1980): 12). Full acceptance of a scientific theory, as a means for systematisation and prediction, is therefore not belief in the truth of the theory.

As another example, consider moral fictionalism. John Mackie (1977) has suggested that our ordinary moral discourse and belief is based on the notion that there are objective moral values. If there are such values, then whether (e.g.) cloning of human beings is wrong or permissible is something that obtains quite independently of what we think. If there are objective values, it would be possible for cloning to be morally wrong even if there were widespread agreement that it is permissible. There would be moral facts, whether or not we were aware of them. But, argues Mackie, there are no objective values (Mackie (1977): 15). Such values would be 'queer', as he puts it. This queerness has more than one aspect. First, since objective values are defined as existing independently of our minds, and yet presumably would not count as part of the fabric of the concrete world, there is a problem of how we could know about them. Second, it is quite unclear how such objective values would be intrinsically motivating: what is it that connects the fact that a certain action is good with our being motivated to perform it? In contrast, a subjectivist account of moral values as being the sort of things we project onto actions as a result of our affective response to them does not raise either problem: there is no puzzle over how we can be aware of our own affective responses or why those responses motivate us to act in certain ways. Insofar as moral subjectivism is correct, and yet our ordinary moral thinking treats moral values as objective, we are in error. Perhaps, however, it is a useful error, for it may sustain certain practices which are socially beneficial. Our natural inclination towards moral objectivism, then, may be vindicated by the instrumental value of the behaviour it elicits. Recognising this, someone who accepts Mackie's arguments (or at least some argument or other) against objective moral values may nevertheless want to continue to accept moral judgements – but that acceptance could no longer be regarded as truth-normed.

Kalderon's characterisation of fictionalism is intended as setting a minimum condition. The label 'fictionalism' suggests that fiction is somehow playing a role in the various fictionalist positions. But it appears to be playing very little role in van Fraassen's constructive empiricism. The constructive empiricist is not playing a game of make-believe with scientific theories. Their truth is not insulated from the external world. Nor is the assertion of those theories merely pretend assertion. Van Fraassen's view of scientific theories is realist, as we have defined realism. But truth, for the constructive empiricist, is not what matters in doing science. What matters is empirical adequacy, and false theories can be empirically adequate, just as true ones are. What justifies calling this position 'fictionalist' is at most an *analogy* with fiction: acceptance of a scientific theory is not truth-normed, just as pretence in a game of make-believe is not truth-normed.

What of moral fictionalism? Is fiction playing an important role here? Richard Joyce (2005) begins his account of moral fictionalism by quoting Mackie's remark that the objectivication of moral values is a 'useful fiction'

(Mackie (1977): 239). But, as Joyce goes on to argue, morality, for the fiction-alist, need not involve sustained pretence. As he puts it:

> The decision to adopt morality as a fiction is best thought of as a kind of precommitment. It is not being suggested that someone enters a shop, is tempted to steal, decides to adopt morality as a fiction, and thus sustains her prudent though faltering decision not to steal. Rather, the resolution to accept the moral point of view is something that occurred in the person's past, and is now an accustomed way of thinking. Its role is that when entering a shop the possibility of stealing doesn't even enter her mind. If a knave were to say to her 'Why not steal?' she would answer without hesitation 'No! – stealing is wrong.' What goes through her mind may be exactly what goes through the mind of the sincere moral believer – it need not 'feel' like make-believe at all (and thus it may have the same influence on behaviour as a belief). (Joyce (2005): 306)

In critical mode, the moral fictionalist will admit that there are no objective values, but nevertheless defend her tendency to acquiesce in natural, realist moral thinking in ordinary contexts. The moral fictionalist can say of moral attitudes – as the constructive empiricist says of scientific theories – that truth does not matter. This could be combined with a realist account of moral discourse or with a subjectivist account. Here again we seem to have at most an analogy with fiction.

Now let's turn to religious fictionalism. The view we find in Braithwaite is, I would contend, fictionalist in a much more full-blooded sense than is suggested by either scientific or moral fictionalism. Two aspects in particular are note-worthy. First, the position Braithwaite articulates is clearly not realist. The religious narratives (in which category the fictionalist will include the more obviously doctrinal elements) are *not* to be taken as attempts to describe the world as it really is, but rather how it is in the fiction. That is a clear point of contrast with constructive empiricism about science. We would not expect Braithwaite's fictionalist to lose sight of the fact that the religious narrative is fiction, even when fully immersed in it. Second, the mechanism by which the religious fiction motivates behaviour is, on Braithwaite's account, causal: the fiction elicits the relevant affective response, which then makes salient the moral reasons for action and enhances their motivational force. That provides a point of contrast with Joyce's moral fictionalist above, for whom moral attitudes (when not interrogated) have the same effect as beliefs and so rationalise the resulting behaviour in a way in which fiction cannot. The more full-blooded form of fictionalism seems more appropriate to the religious case as there is much more for the imagination to get to work with than either the moral or the scientific case, where the relevant subject is to do with unobservables.

By way of further contrast, recall from Section 1 the position labelled 'non-doxasticism' (short for non-doxastic religious realism). The non-doxasticist accepts religious statements, but this attitude is distinct from belief. Bearing in mind Kalderon's distinction between full and tentative acceptance, the kind of non-doxasticist who accepts religious statements on an experimental basis, while continuing to care whether or not they are actually true, will not count as a fictionalist, even in a minimal sense. That is because, although the attitude towards any given religious statement will not be truth-normed, it is part of a wider understanding of religious statements as answerable to the facts. This kind of non-doxasticist is essentially agnostic about religious statements. To count as a fictionalist, the religious non-doxasticist would have to cease to regard the actual truth of religious statements as religiously important. (For a discussion of what we might call different grades or strengths of religious fictionalism, see Deng (2015).)

From now on, then, I shall take religious fictionalism to be the view that to immerse oneself in the religion, to employ its discourse to express that immersion, and to allow it to influence (in part via the emotional responses it evokes) is to engage in a game of make-believe. In that (entirely serious) game, to utter religious statements is not assert them, but to pretend to assert them. That is why neither the fictionalist's utterances, not the attitudes they convey, are truth-normed.

The position which Peter Lipton (2007) recommends is, I think, a fairly full-blooded fictionalism about religion, despite the fact that he models it on constructive empiricism. He does, however, draw attention to the following significant difference between the two. The constructive empiricist uses scientific theories to generate observational predictions, and to these predictions the appropriate attitude is truth-normed. Moreover the warrant to believe in the truth of the predictions is that they follow from theories which have passed empirical tests. Religious texts do not provide warrant for believing anything, but they do, as Braithwaite argued, induce attitudes which are warranted on other, non-religious, grounds. (Lipton's aim, incidentally, is to reconcile religious attitudes with trust in the deliverances of science, a reconciliation which is achieved by combining scientific realism with religious fictionalism, though Lipton does not employ the word 'fictionalist'. He labels his view the 'immersion solution.')

The religious fictionalist faces a challenge not faced, or at least not faced to the same extent, by moral and scientific fictionalism, and that is finding an appropriate fiction to work with. Braithwaite thinks that this is simply a matter for the individual, who can be entirely unconstrained in their choice of story – indeed, can invent their own. But can the fictionalist enjoy quite so much freedom?

3.2 Whose Fiction?

In his introduction to an edition of the Book of Job, the novelist G. K. Chesterton comments:

> A cosmic philosophy is not constructed to fit a man; a cosmic philosophy is constructed to fit a cosmos. A man can no more possess a private religion than he can possess a private sun and moon. (Chesterton (1916): 9)

The first sentence clearly announces that, in our terms, Chesterton is a realist in matters of religion. And that explains the second sentence. However, if we detach that second sentence from its realist background, there remains an independent motivation, one to exercise the fictionalist. If someone constructs their own fiction, they may be proud of it, they may enjoy contemplating it, they may enter imaginatively into the fiction as a means of extending it further, they may become fond of the central characters. But is it plausible that it could stir such feelings as to be a means for the *moral improvement* of its author? Could it have the kind of emotional, and moral, impact that a fiction created by someone else could have, a fiction that seems to have a life of its own, a fiction whose independence from those who engage with it gives it a kind of objectivity? It seems that the religious fictionalist will be obliged to choose between one of the many available religions.

This in itself is not troubling for the fictionalist, for part of the instrumental value of religion is its role in forming cohesive communities, unified by a common discourse and a common set of ideals (Eshleman (2005)). Adopting a religious tradition identifies one with a particular religious community. So the selection of any given religion is much more likely to be determined by cultural factors than anything else. Only one religion may in practice be a live contender. (This is not to deny what is plainly the case, namely that people occasionally move from one religion to another, but typically this happens for decidedly non-fictionalist reasons.) And it is important, for instrumental reasons, that one religious fiction is chosen. Imagine a fictionalist who simply moves at whim from one religion to another. It is hard to see that this involves anything other than a very provisional, and perhaps also superficial, commitment to the religious life. In contrast, a fictionalist who stays true to a particular religious fiction is in a better position to explore it more deeply, to let it guide them more thoroughly.

However, if the argument from historical intention outlined in Section 1 is based on a correct assumption, the fictionalist, as well as making use of the obviously fictional stories which are part of a religious tradition, is also appropriating narratives and ideas which were not originally intended as fictional.

(And there is a difference, as Cordry (2010) notes, between *interpreting* a discourse, which is sensitive to the intentions of those using it, and *appropriating* it, which may not be so sensitive.) They only become fictional when the fictionalist intentionally incorporates them into the fiction. So there is a sense in which the fictionalist's religion is private: the story, *as* a story, has to be sustained by the fictionalist's own intentions.

As for the interpretation of the stories, the fictionalist can exercise a degree of choice, but not an excessive amount if they are to remain within the religious community. They may take the basic religious narrative as a trunk from which may sprout different fictional branches, corresponding to different ways in which the narrative might be developed. Engaging with the fiction might involve a certain amount of hopping from branch to branch. We do not need to prioritise one branch over another. (Though, bearing in mind the reasons given above against the practice of a fickle fictionalism that simply moves through different religious traditions, the hopping should not get out of hand.)

Having, I hope, given a little more detail to the basic core of the fictionalist account we find in Braithwaite's discussion, let us consider how successfully the fictionalist can engage in the religious life, starting with their integration into the religious community. And it is now time to introduce our two heroes.

3.3 The Fictionalist in the Community: a Shared Language?

Reginald and Fiona are regular churchgoers. They sing hymns, join in prayers, discuss the sermon afterwards and often meet to read passages of the Bible together and explore the meanings and implications of those passages. They seem to the neutral onlooker to be equally engaged in these activities, equally inspired by them, and equally inclined to relate them to their everyday lives. Behaviourally, then, there is nothing to distinguish the religious attitudes of these two individuals. However, on questioning, each gives a very different philosophical account of the basis of that behaviour:

Reginald is a *realist*, and more specifically he is a realist *believer*. In terms of the categories introduced in Section 1, he is a doxastic religious realist. He takes God-talk – subject to an important qualification – at face-value, and as true by virtue of the way the world is independently of human belief. He takes statements about God to refer to a real, mind-independent being. The important qualification is that this face-value approach applies to the most central statements of his religion, including the doctrinal statements. He recognises that a significant proportion of scripture is metaphorical, or couched in terms of stories and parables. He is a realist, but not a fundamentalist.

Fiona is a *fictionalist*. When engaging in religious language and practice, she takes herself to be engaging in a (rather complex) game of make-believe. When she utters 'God loves us', for example, this is pretend assertion rather than assertion. However, it is well-motivated pretence. It is not a cynical attempt to deceive in order to gain by illicit means the more obvious benefits of being part of a religious community. Rather, she wishes to enter into what she takes to be the religious imagination to the extent that she becomes affectively engaged, and so more inclined to lead the kind of life she has independent reason for leading. She also takes her utterances to be constrained, to a large extent, by the content of her chosen religion. It is appropriate to pretend certain things, not appropriate to pretend others.

We might imagine the history of the interactions between Reginald and Fiona being divided into two phases: before they become aware of their radically different interpretations of the nature of theological discourse, and afterwards, when each confesses to the other what they take the nature and point of the discourse to be. But how different would the two phases be? We might suppose that, perhaps after the initial surprise (at least on Reginald's part), the friends decide that there is no reason why they should not continue exactly as before, since the differences between them are not so much religious as *meta*-religious. That is, they concern issues that arise when we reflect on religious activity, as opposed to participating in it. Such meta-religious issues will concern questions about the content, justification, or role of religious language, beliefs or practices. Recognising that, in any case, there will be, within any religious community, divergence of views of one sort or another, the friends feel that a spirit of philosophical ecumenism is called for, and that this diversity of interpretative perspectives is likely to enhance rather than undermine their religiously motivated interactions with each other. Such, at any rate, is their hope.

We may wonder, however, how far this spirit of philosophical ecumenism can prevail. Can a religious community in which realist belief represents the dominant outlook accommodate fictionalists? We might expect the common ground between realists and fictionalists to be relatively limited and the state of peaceful co-existence between them to be only on the surface, concealing deeper disagreements. After all, whereas the realists are genuinely trying to make contact with a transcendent being, the fictionalists are merely playing the God game. Are these sceptical doubts justified?

On the face of it, Fiona and Reginald have a lot in common, making it relatively easy for them to maintain their policy of peaceful co-existence. Both agree that statements made in the language of God-talk are the sort of statements that can be true or false. They are not merely expressions of emotion or behavioural commitments, for example. Nor are they coded assertions about certain kinds of experience. They agree on the decision procedures for deciding which statements it is appropriate to make: appeals to scripture, to canonical statements of doctrine, and to the implications of these. They may even both appeal to considerations of natural theology: the project of relating theological truth to natural phenomena. Natural theology is typically presented as a realist enterprise. But there is no reason why a fictionalist cannot incorporate the same kind of project, for the religious fiction is not isolated from the real world. Features of the actual world – the fine-tuning of the universe, for example – can be incorporated into the religious fiction, and play a role within it. And indeed our understanding of ordinary fiction is almost always informed by knowledge of how things are in fact. A rudimentary understanding of the world's actual geography, for example, is a requisite for following the narrative of Jules Verne's *Around the World in Eighty Days*. Similarly, an understanding of actual Tudor history will enrich a reading of Hilary Mantel's *Wolf Hall* and similar historical novels. The authors of such novels will incorporate quite a bit of the relevant history, but some of this background readers might supply for ourselves, particularly if they are minded to extend the events of the novel in their own imagination. Such extension is precisely what the fictionalist about religious discourse may wish to engage in. So Fiona need not absent herself from conversations with Reginald about natural theology.

Nor need Fiona insist that Reginald is mistaken about the factual content of the statements he utters. For if fictional discourse requires fictive intention, Reginald, who has no such intention, cannot be mistaken in taking *his* statements to be objectively fact-stating. (He would, however, be mistaken if he extended that understanding to the statements made by Fiona.)

Both, too, can give religious discourse a central role in shaping their moral and spiritual outlook. Seeing the world through the interpretative framework of God-centred discourse allows them both to get more clearly in focus what is of most value in life: love for others, displacement of the self from the centre of one's projects, the voice of conscience, the subordination of short-term goals for long-term ones, etc. None of this is inaccessible from the atheistic perspective – it would be arrogant to suggest otherwise – but it is much more accessible (argue Reginald and Fiona) if one inhabits the theistic framework.

Is the appearance of genuine communication between Reginald and Fiona entirely genuine, however? Statements uttered by Reginald will certainly *sound* the same as statements uttered by Fiona, and there will be a significant number of forms of words to which they are both prepared to give utterance. But the intended function of a statement as uttered by Reginald, and that of an apparently identical one as uttered by Fiona, will be quite different. The realist's talk of God either refers to a real, transcendent being or it simply fails to refer. The fictionalist's talk of God, in contrast, refers to a fictional character, and, given the framework, it cannot fail to do so. Different functions, it might be suggested, different content, and so no genuine communication. On the other hand, it is quite implausible to suggest that sentences have completely different meanings depending on whether they occur in a fictional or non-fictional context. 'The cat is on the mat', as uttered by a fictional character, conjures up the same image in the mind of the reader as that same sentence uttered in real life. We do not need a translation manual to be able to read a novel written in our own language. Statements about a cat in a fictional context really do represent a cat (just a purely imaginary one). And any doubts that Reginald and Fiona are using words to mean the same things can be put to rest by checking that they both agree on the inferential patterns exhibited by God statements. Both agree, for example, that 'God spoke to Moses' entails 'God spoke to someone.' In the context of specific theories of meaning, admittedly, the meaning of 'Fire!', as uttered in a burning building, will not be the same as the meaning of 'Fire!', as uttered by an actor on stage. If we apply Herbert Grice's (1957) theory of meaning, for example, we will understand the first in terms of what the utterer wants us to believe, the second in terms of what the author wants us to imagine. But there will be a very significant, and asymmetric, connection. As we might put it, the meaning in a fictional context is parasitic on the meaning in a non-fictional context. It is because a non-fictional utterance of 'Fire!' means what it does that a fictional utterance of 'Fire!' means what *it* does.

The apparent robustness of the agreement between Reginald and Fiona, then, provides some hope that fictionalists can be integrated into a predominantly realist community. But can the fictionalist fully engage with the religious life? We will examine three characteristic aspects of such a life (characteristic, at least, of some paradigmatic religions). They are: reciting creeds, prayer (especially private prayer), and the emotional basis of religious behaviour.

3.4 Creed and Prayer

'I believe in God, the Father Almighty, Maker of Heaven and Earth.' We have come to the point in a religious service – Anglican Evensong will serve as our example – where all turn to the altar and recite the Apostles' Creed. What is going on here? If these words are uttered by a doxastic religious realist like Reginald, what is going on is exactly what seems to be going on: the realist is expressing their belief in a transcendent being, involving not just assent to the existence of such a being, but also trust in that being. For the non-doxastic realist, in contrast, these words express some kind of acceptance as opposed to belief. And for both of these realists, part of the speech act of reciting the Creed may also be a commitment to a certain course of action implied by the content of the Creed. For the conative expressivist (of a rather pure kind, one who does not combine this view with any other), this commitment to action is the whole of what is expressed. But for Fiona? The obvious answer here is that reciting creeds is part of the game of make-believe, and that what is going on here is a pretence: the fictionalist does not actually believe, but is pretending to express belief.

If this seems more questionable than the fictionalist's engagement with other aspects of the service (singing hymns and psalms, listening to the readings, saying the prayers), it is perhaps precisely because the words 'I believe' put the spotlight on the individual and seem to be designed precisely to strip away all pretence. This is likely to be the line the realist would take. But the fictionalist will insist that reciting the creeds cannot be separated from these other activities in this way: they are part of an integrated whole. The spirit in which the fictionalist says 'I believe' is no less sincere than the spirit in which they participate in any other part of the liturgy. The realist may reply that, though this is no doubt true, it is only so because the whole of the fictionalist's participation is insincere! But sincerity is to be judged according to the intentions of the participant. If those intentions are to deceive, to enjoy the benefits of a society whose principles one secretly rejects, then this is indeed insincere. But if it is a means to moral and spiritual improvement, to the benefit of all, it is not.

Arguably, it is the agnostic non-doxasticist who has the harder time here, as there is no pretence in their case, so we are left with more of a conflict between the meaning of the words and the attitude expressed. However, both fictionalist and non-doxasticist can agree that, although the meaning of the words is not given by the commitment to action, the state of mind in which one utters the creeds is one which prepares one to undertake that commitment. It is that commitment, which is entirely genuine, that separates them from the exploitative cynic, who is merely giving lip service to the creeds.

What now of prayer? Public prayer is, like the creeds, an integral part of the service and so for Fiona the fictionalist, this will also be part of the make-believe. Saying prayers in this context is a performance, in which Fiona pretends (though not as an act of deception) to address a transcendent being. But what about when we move from the public arena to a private one? In an act of public worship, and perhaps particularly when a significant number of those participating are realists, the fictionalist will be caught up in the solemnity, joyfulness and intensity of the occasion. It is comparatively easy, in those circumstances, to engage fully with the fiction (as the fictionalist sees it). But public worship does not exhaust the repertoire of religious practices: there is also the time spent in private prayer, time to which the realist would attach considerable value and importance. How will the fictionalist approach private prayer?

Let's consider first the reasons Reginald might have for engaging in private prayer. First, he may use it to petition God for various things he desires, in the hope that God will grant his requests. Second, he may use it for companionship, to help him feel closer to God. Third, he may use it for something intermediate between these: to align his will with the will of God. By coming closer to God in prayer, he hopes to become aware of the divine will, and in so doing reorient, as far as possible, his own desires.

Can any of these have a counterpart in Fiona's outlook? The first, prayer as petition, seems ruled out at once. Fiona cannot but be aware that no-one is there to grant her requests, and the attempt to make such a request will surely strike her as a sham. There can be no willing suspension of belief here. But this may not be the loss it appears. After all, even realists may have reason to be suspicious of petitionary prayer. Can we really ask God to intervene if he does not already judge it appropriate to do so? Either what will happen, without intervention, is already in accordance with what he ordains, in which case intervention will make things worse, or it is not in accordance with the divine will, but intervention would not be compatible with the desire to allow humans to shape the world by their own unaided actions. (See, e.g., Basinger (1983).) And in any case, the realist may take the view that petitionary prayer is something we should grow out of. Rather than asking God to fix things, as if we were children, we should rather see ourselves as the instruments of God's purpose. So although Fiona cannot, without a serious degree of self-deception, replicate the realist's use of petitionary prayer, this may not be such a problem from the mature religious viewpoint.

What of the second use of prayer, the seeking after companionship? For Fiona, there is no companion, and praying as if there is, for the sake of companionship, invites comparison with the sad case of someone's picking up the telephone and (trying to ignore the dialling tone) having a pretend, and very one-sided, conversation, in the vain hope that they will feel a little less lonely. Surely, then, this second use of prayer can have no genuine counterpart in Fiona's life.

That might seem to rule out the third use of prayer, too: the aligning of one's will with the will of God. There is no (real) will of God if there is no (real) God. But might one nevertheless attempt to align one's will with what one imagines *would be* the will of God? Fictional character though he may be, God represents for Fiona a moral ideal, an expression of perfect love. There is nothing self-deceptive in Fiona's genuine attempt to order her will in accordance with this ideal. But then, it will be objected, there is no need for Fiona to do this through the medium of prayer. All she need do is to contemplate that ideal and attempt to order her desires accordingly. There is no need for a fake attempt at communication. Nevertheless, Fiona may find that a cool contemplation of an ideal is not sufficient. She needs to enter more imaginatively into a vision of pure love. Prayer might just be the medium for that imaginative state. It is not an act of communication, and indeed it need not take precisely that form. It might, rather, be a meditation and one in which Fiona might find it helpful to voice, in her head, her own thoughts, as if they were addressed to another person, and imagine what someone motivated only by love would say in response. And, without there being any actually hallucinatory experience, answers may come to her as if they did not have their origin in her own thoughts. Phenomenologically, this could have a great deal in common with the experience of prayer that many realists have.

There is one other aspect of prayer that might come under this third heading, which the fictionalist cannot wholly replicate, and that is the wrestling with doubt that even the staunchest realist is subject to from time to time. 'Help thou mine unbelief', cries the realist (Mark 9:24). Fiona is not subject to those doubts, since they cannot arise in the fictionalist framework. Is this a loss? Reginald might argue that this wrestling with doubt is part of the authentic religious experience, something that sharpens one's awareness of the demands of a religious life, and a constant test of the sincerity of one's faith. That this should find no counterpart in Fiona's life makes hers a less truly religious outlook. But perhaps, after all, there is a counterpart in Fiona's prayers. There is a cognitive dissonance that threatens the fictionalist's religious engagement. Awareness of the fictional nature of what is being said and appealed to may at any time break in upon Fiona's sincere attempt to immerse herself in the fiction. Dealing with that dissonance, resisting its disruptive effect, bears some comparison to the realist's attempt to cope with doubt. Further, Fiona's loyalty to her chosen fiction may be tested from time to time, when it confronts her with uncomfortable moral, psychological or spiritual truths, and on those occasions some effort of will is required not simply to abandon it.

3.5 Religious Attitudes, Emotion and the Paradox of Fiction

As we saw in the previous section, in our discussion of Braithwaite, another potential difference between realism and fictionalism is the role religious attitudes play in the shaping of behaviour. For Reginald, religious beliefs stand in a reason-giving relation to moral attitudes. For example, the belief that God loves us provides a reason to love each other: we are objectively lovable! But since Fiona only fictionally believes that God loves us, her attitude cannot be reason-providing in the same way since the *fictional* truth that God loves us does not give us a reason actually to love each other. No merely fictional truth, it seems, can give us a reason to do anything. It does not help to point out that it is fictionally true that 'the fact that God loves us gives us a reason to love each other', for again what counts as a reason in the fiction has no implications for moral attitudes outside the fiction.

This is not to deny that engaging with fiction can shape and develop our moral understanding. Indeed this is part of its very considerable value. But more than one mechanism is at work. First, a fiction might alert us to certain truths about human nature (the characters will not, typically, be presented as having a wholly alien mentality), or present us with hypothetical dilemmas which test our moral understanding. In fiction, then, we may indeed find reasons for what we do – but then those reasons aren't (or aren't wholly) fictional truths. Second, at a somewhat more immediate level, we find ourselves emotionally involved with the fictional characters. Notoriously, our anxiety, joy and sadness for them seem to sit side by side with a firm belief that they do not actually exist. That emotional involvement may then go on to alter our behaviour towards real people, in positive ways. Here, as Braithwaite pointed out, the relation between fictional truth is not so much reason-giving but causal. Or since (as Davidson (1963) plausibly argued) reasons can also be causes, we should avoid the implication that reasons are acausal, and say just that fiction shapes our behaviour in ways that don't appeal to reasons, through the emotions.

A third mechanism may also be in operation. If the model of fictionalist prayer outlined in the previous section is viable, then it suggests a further route whereby engaging with the fiction may lead to action, other than the purely causal route via emotional responses appealed to by Braithwaite. Perhaps the religious fiction can be reason-providing, by getting us to contemplate relevant counterfactuals. The 'practical syllogism' the fictionalist constructs is something like this: 'In this situation, I should do whatever a perfectly loving being would do. A perfectly loving being (were it to exist) would do x. Therefore I should do x.'

The second mechanism, involving the emotions, is one which should be both recognised and exploited by the realist. Reginald, who is, recall, no fundamentalist, accepts that many (though not all) of the narratives of his religion are stories, parables, images – in other words, fictions, though important fictions. So there will be significant overlap between his response to the narratives and Fiona's: both involve an emotional response to what they nevertheless recognise as fictional, and both have behavioural consequences.

But it may be thought, nonetheless, that Fiona is rather more reliant on this means of motivating religious behaviour than Reginald, who can also appeal to his religious beliefs to rationalise religious behaviour. And so the problem known in aesthetics as the 'paradox of fiction' (see Radford (1975), Lamarque (1981), Matravers (1997)) poses more of a threat to Fiona's engagement in the religious life than to Reginald's. To explain: the paradox of fiction arises as a result of the tension between the following plausible propositions:

1. We respond emotionally to certain fictional states of affairs, even when recognising that they are purely fictional.
2. Emotional responses to states of affairs depend on the belief that those states really obtain.

Both of these are backed by evidence: fictions which are presented *as* fictions undoubtedly evoke emotions such as joy, sadness, anxiety, wistfulness, terror, and so on. And yet a change in emotional state seems to be accompanied by a change in belief state (think of anxiety turning to relief when the dreaded event is known to have passed). It seems that either one of these propositions has to go, or they need to be qualified so that they no longer come into conflict. We could reject 1 on the grounds that emotional responses to fiction involve suppression of the belief that it is fiction – the 'suspension of disbelief', in Coleridge's phrase (Schaper (1978)). But if we hold this while retaining 2, then we have to say that when emotionally enthralled by fiction, we not only suspend disbelief, we also actually believe that the fictional events are real. Not only does this seem too strong a thesis, but we then lack an explanation of why we don't behave as we would ordinarily do when we believe a state of affairs obtains – why, for instance, we don't run from the cinema when some murderous creature appears on the screen.

Kendall Walton's approach is, in effect, to modify both propositions (Walton (1978)). The affective states generated by fictions, he suggests, are only 'quasi-emotions': they exhibit some of the qualitative and physiological characteristics of genuine emotions, but are not the full-blown article, and this is why they do not lead to the actions associated with genuine emotion. In support of Walton's solution, we might point to the fact that many people clearly enjoy watching horror films, despite the fact that they portray scenes which, if taken to be real, would not be remotely enjoyable.

Still, the existence of quasi-emotions has to be explained. If not by belief, then what? One suggestion is that emotions are sometimes evoked by perceptual input which is only partially processed: there is a mental representation of a state of affairs, indeed, but this falls short of belief. Tamar Szabo Gendler (2008) has suggested the name 'alief' for the representational state in question. Someone walking on a glass floor suspended above a yawning drop may be exhibiting the characteristic physiological signs of fear: raised heartbeat, respiratory rate, perspiration, and so on. They may also report feeling afraid, yet also profess the belief that they are in no danger at all. In this particular case, a plausible explanation is that some autonomic responses are triggered by perceptual input, without the need for the mediation of conscious states. Now, admittedly, this case is one where a fairly basic level of processing is involved, and it would not be plausible to suggest that the emotional response to fiction is nothing more than reflex autonomic responses to perceptual cues. A rather more sophisticated level of cognitive processing seems to be taking place here. Nevertheless, perceptual cues such as those of someone in distress, say, might well trigger a natural sympathetic response: we might imagine various levels of information processing which, though conscious, operate below the threshold of belief. 'Alief' could be applied to a whole range of representational states which fall short of belief. And the nature of the emotional state induced, ranging from an automatic fear reflex to empathy with the portrayal of a character on stage, could well reflect the kind of alief which induces it.

Supposing that something like this approach is an appropriate response to the paradox of fiction, there will remain the worry that the fictionalist's emotional responses to the religious stories will be qualitatively different from the realist's, simply because they are in a different cognitive state. Both Fiona and Reginald respond emotionally to something they both recognise as fiction, but for Reginald the response is likely to be coloured by the background belief in the underlying religious narrative. Is there a danger that the fictionalist's emotional responses will be religiously inappropriate? We can illustrate this by means of a problem that is related to the paradox of fiction: the paradox of tragedy, memorably articulated by David Hume. In his essay 'Of Tragedy' he writes:

> It seems an unaccountable pleasure, which the spectators of a well-written tragedy receive from sorrow, terror, anxiety, and other passions, that are in themselves disagreeable and uneasy. The more they are touched and affected, the more are they delighted with the spectacle; and as soon as the uneasy passions cease to operate, the piece is at an end ... They are pleased in proportion as they are afflicted, and never are so happy as when they employ tears, sobs, and cries to give vent to their sorrow, and relieve their heart, swoln with the tenderest sympathy and compassion. (Hume (1757): 237)

What would be wholly negative emotions if the scenes witnessed were taken to be real may be pleasurable and sought after in the context of fiction. Aestheticians are concerned to explain this phenomenon, and here the qualitative difference between the emotions invoked by alief and those evoked by the corresponding belief may provide a possible answer. But whatever the explanation is, we can frame the phenomenon as a problem for fictionalism. Some religious narratives involve scenes of suffering that should stir the strongest negative emotions, for example, the Christian passion narrative in which God the Son, incarnate in Jesus Christ, is interrogated, tormented and put to one of the cruellest deaths imaginable. Insofar as realists will take this to be the unvarnished truth, their grief and sorrow will be appropriate to the content of the narrative. But what of the fictionalist? (I am assuming, for the sake of the example, a wholly fictionalist interpretation of the narrative, setting aside the evidence we have for historical events which correspond at least in part with that narrative.) As fiction, it has the marks of tragedy – though not just those. The risk then is that the fiction will generate something like the reaction Hume describes. But this would surely be out of place. The proper religious response should be one of appalled horror and sorrow, not a frisson of horrified delight.

If there is a difficulty here, realists are not immune to it. For religious narratives, even when viewed realistically, are often presented in a dramatic, artistic or musical medium which exploits aesthetic features which cannot but evoke pleasurable emotions: consider the York mystery plays, the religious paintings of William Blake, Handel's Messiah or Bach's St Matthew and St John Passions. If these can be enjoyed as artworks – as they plainly are – does this interfere with the proper religious response? Whatever the realist has to say here in defence of such artworks may also serve the fictionalist.

3.6 The Moral Seriousness of Religious Realism

Creeds, prayers, the use of religious narrative as a spur to action: all these are cited by Reginald as cases where the realist has a properly serious approach to the religious life. We have offered above ways in which the fictionalist can respond, but the impression may remain that the fictionalist can partake at best only in a faint shadow of the realist's religious life. However, in what is evidently one of their less ecumenical exchanges, Fiona retorts that it is actually Reginald who exhibits a lack of seriousness, in particular, a lack of *moral* seriousness. She makes out her case as follows: true moral seriousness in religion requires not merely conformity to that religion's moral code, and not just in addition an internalisation of those principles, so that one is naturally inclined to follow them. It also requires critical reflection on those principles, and the conclusion that those are indeed the principles to follow, that they are recommended by one's own independently-arrived-at outlook. Reginald, in contrast, is taking a shortcut to this conclusion: it is (really) God's will that I act in this way, therefore I must act in this way, whether or not I recognise any independent reasons for acting in this way.

Braithwaite, I think, would not himself recognise a contrast between realist and fictionalist here, for he thinks that even if it is *believed* that a certain course of action is the will of God, that is not sufficient reason to take that course of action, for 'it is when the religious man finds that what the magnified Lord Shaftesbury commands or desires accords with his own moral judgement that he decides to obey or to accede to it' (Braithwaite (1955): 89. This is an allusion to Matthew Arnold's analogy of the Trinity in terms of three versions of Lord Shaftesbury, the Victorian reformer.). It is not clear that Braithwaite is right about this. Surely the religious realist *would* regard the fact that God commands a certain action as an overriding reason to perform that action. There is the issue of how one would know that God commands it, and perhaps the promptings of his conscience would tell Reginald that this is God's will. If so, it is not the promptings of conscience by themselves that provide the primary reason for performing the action, but rather because they intimate the will of God. We can, however, agree that what Brathwaite says of the believer here applies to the fictionalist, and so it is not a problem that religious stories, if viewed as stories, cannot rationalise the behaviour they motivate.

What Reginald is guilty of, Fiona continues, is in effect an abdication of a second-order moral responsibility: the responsibility for working out one's own moral responsibilities for oneself rather than relying on some external source. There is, therefore, an element of passivity to Reginald's morality, which contrasts unfavourably with Fiona's own autonomy. Naturally, Fiona does not put it in quite such uncompromising terms to the thoughtful and self-critical Reginald, but isn't there a danger of realist religion becoming morally infanti-lising if the realist isn't very careful? Both appeal to religious narratives, but for Fiona this is not a source of knowledge; rather it is a device which reinforces behaviour through the emotions. It is not in any sense a substitute for moral thinking.

Reginald will doubtless object that this quite unfairly underestimates the degree of moral reflection that – of course! – he brings to bear on the religious narratives. The moral imperatives he derives from his religion are *indeed* those that coincide with his own judgement. But what, urges Fiona, if he found that there was some conflict? Would it not then be a case of 'Not my will, but thy will be done'? That is, there must be a subordination of one's independent moral judgement to that which emerges from the narratives, a giving up of one's moral autonomy that is quite absent from her own religious life.

Fiona and Reginald are unlikely to agree on which of them is the more serious, morally speaking, in their approach to religion. But what this exchange shows is that it cannot be taken for granted that it is the fictionalist who lags behind, who has to accept second best when it comes to the interaction between religion and morality.

4 Fictionalism and Evil

> The riddles of God are more satisfying than the solutions of man.
> G. K. Chesterton, *Introduction to the Book of Job* (1916)

4.1 Do Fictionalists Face a Problem of Evil?

Before defining the problem for fictionalism, let us begin by rehearsing the two main versions of the problem of evil – or, if you prefer, two problems of evil – as they arise for the realist. To express the problem in its most basic terms: there are, without question, instances of the most appalling suffering in the world, including the suffering of non-human animals. Can we square this indisputable fact with the existence of God, as traditionally conceived? Since God so conceived is omniscient (all-knowing), God knows about this suffering. Since God so conceived is omnipotent (all-powerful), he could prevent this suffering if he wanted to. And since God (again, so conceived) is both perfectly loving and perfectly good, he would indeed want to prevent this suffering. But now we seem to have a contradiction: he knows about it, can prevent it, wants to prevent it, and yet does not. This is the *logical problem of evil*: the existence of suffering is incompatible with the existence of God, traditionally conceived (Mackie (1982): Ch. 9).

To answer the problem, thus expressed, religious realists may appeal to two strategies: *defences*, which show simply that there need be no logical incompatibility between the existence of God and the existence of suffering, and *theodicies*, which attempt to provide a plausible account of how suffering could be part of God's design for humanity. An example of a defence would be the *free will defence*: God made us free beings, but as free beings, we sometimes choose evil, and suffering is the result (Plantinga (1977)). An example of a theodicy would be the *soul-making theodicy*: through suffering we learn to be truly compassionate beings and capable of taking moral responsibility for our actions (Hick (2007)). The problem with both defences and theodicies is the apparent existence of *gratuitous* suffering: suffering which cannot be explained away through any of the proposed models. The suffering that results from natural disasters does not appear to be a consequence of the exercise of free will. And some suffering is so acute that, so far from building souls, it appears to destroy them, producing individuals who are so damaged they are unable to become full moral agents. Putting these considerations together, and making all assumptions explicit, we can now state the logical problem in a somewhat fuller form. The following constitute an inconsistent set of propositions:

(1) There exists a being, God, who is omniscient, omnipotent, perfectly good, perfectly loving and perfectly rational.
(2) If God is omniscient, then God knows both of any actual suffering and of what suffering would result from any given situation were he not to prevent it.
(3) If God is omnipotent, then God is able to prevent any instance of suffering.
(4) If God is perfectly loving, then God would prevent, if he was able to, any suffering which could not be justified in terms of the divine plan.
(5) If God is both perfectly good and perfectly rational, then the divine plan is wholly good.
(6) There exists suffering which could not be justified in terms of any plan which was wholly good.

To briefly motivate each of these: (1) is of course the traditional theistic view. (2) follows from the definition of omniscience in terms of knowing all truths. (3) follows from the definition of omnipotence in terms of a capacity to bring about any logically possible state of affairs, given that the absence of any instance of suffering is logically possible. (4) follows from the assumption that being perfectly loving would entail wanting what is good for creation. (5) follows from the assumption that a wholly good, rational being would devise a plan which would maximise the chances of achieving what is good for creation (an irrational being could not be trusted to do so, even if they were entirely benevolent).

The vulnerable point for the theist, assuming the traditional conception of deity, is (6). Certainly, there *appears* to be suffering which could not be justified, but how much insight can we expect to have into the divine will? Much of God's nature and understanding is perforce hidden from us. An intellectual humility proper to religious realism would surely allow that there is a justification for suffering, even apparently gratuitous suffering, which lies beyond our current understanding. The realist may, at this point as at many others, appeal to the mysteriousness of the divine. This might go together with an acceptance of one of the available theodicies. In this case, the idea is that, although we have a viable account of the kind of consideration which would justify even apparently gratuitous suffering, we do not have a grasp of the detailed justification of particular instances of such suffering. This strategy is known as 'sceptical theism' (see McBrayer (2010) for discussion). Or the appeal to mysteriousness might be more wide-ranging and go together with a rejection of the theodicies proposed so far. The idea here might be that such theodicies are unsatisfactory because they trivialise, or at least under-estimate, the suffering that there is. Nevertheless, there exists *some* theodicy, beyond our mental and emotional reach.

However, although this may relieve some internal pressure in the world-view of the believer, it is likely to have less appeal to someone taking a more neutral viewpoint. If you are undecided whether or not to believe in God, the existence of suffering for which you are unable to imagine an adequate justification will serve as evidence against the existence of God. This is the *evidential problem of evil* (Rowe (1978)). Perhaps it is possible that there is a wholly good divine plan on which such suffering as we see is justified, but we struggle to see what such a plan would look like.

So concludes a very brief sketch of the familiar lines of debate over the problem(s) of evil. Now let us put it in a fictionalist context. Braithwaite clearly envisaged the fictionalist as being able to exercise a considerable degree of freedom in adapting whatever religious fiction best supported their moral and spiritual development. But, as we suggested in the previous section, the choice of religious fiction will in part be determined by cultural factors. And if the fiction-alist wishes to be integrated into a religious community in which realism is dominant, they will not take too many liberties over the central narratives. An eclectic fictionalist is likely to be a marginalised fictionalist. So let us envisage a theological fiction in which God is conceived along traditional lines. (And fictionalist versions of the great Abrahamic religions will be likely to include such a conception.) Propositions (1)–(5) will therefore be built into such a fiction. But what of (6)? Here is perhaps a more likely opportunity for the fictionalist to exert their freedom in determining the content of the fiction. Not all facts about the real world need be imported into the fiction. Indeed, many facts will simply be irrelevant: the number of Morris Minors manufactured in 1968, for instance, or the shift in migrating habits of the red-necked grebe over the last two decades, or the odds on England winning the next World Cup, and so on. But the facts of appalling suffering are not, surely, religiously irrelevant. Any fictionalist who excluded such a salient feature of experience simply in order not to disturb their religious fiction would appear to be indulging in escapism rather than engaging with a process of spiritual and moral development. As Jon Robson, who rightly objects to this strategy, has pointed out, it would rule out a religious response to terrible suffering, which in turn would imply that the fictionalist cannot, after all, engage fully in a key element of the religious life (Robson (2015): 356). So how much suffering to include? All of it? Or just enough to develop a religious response to suffering, yet not so much as to conflict with the theological elements of the fiction, including whichever theodicy had been imported into it? But again, there seems to be artificiality in the attempt to avoid conflict. To be morally significant, the religious fiction must incorporate the most salient aspects of life, including not only sources of joy and wonder, but also ones which provoke moral crises. But if (6) is incorporated into the fiction, then we have the logical problem of evil appearing within the fiction. The fiction is, indeed, logically inconsistent.

What if an epistemic counterpart of (6) is incorporated into the fiction instead? A proposition such as:

> (6)* There exists suffering which *we cannot imagine* being justified in terms of any plan which was wholly good.

It is (6)*, or something very like it, that gives rise to the evidential problem of evil. Although (6*) is not logically inconsistent with the existence of an all-powerful, etc., being, it still makes belief in the existence of such a being harder to sustain. So by incorporating (6)* into the fiction, would the fiction-alist thus have incorporated the evidential problem of evil? Having entered into a fiction in which God exists, there is no serious question then of whether God exists or not within the fiction: it is just a given that this is so. We do not go looking for other fictional truths which would justify us in either accepting or not accepting that God exists within the fiction. However, we can reason-ably expect the fiction to be coherent, where this is not simply a matter of logical consistency, but a matter of the various components of the fiction fitting together into a unified picture of the world. A fiction in which there exists a being who is all-powerful, all-knowing and all-loving, but also one in which there is suffering of a kind which would ordinarily be taken as evidence against the existence of such a being, *and* in which there is no adequate explanatory narrative which shows why this being permits that degree of suffering, is one in which there is considerable tension. This, then, is the fictionalist problem of evil. How might the fictionalist respond?

4.2 Avoiding the Problem: a Modified Fiction

Let us return to the two characters introduced in Section 3.3: Reginald the realist and Fiona the fictionalist. What happens when Fiona and Reginald's conversation turns to the problem of evil? Reginald feels some pressure to reconcile his realist belief in the goodness of God with the evident fact of suffering. Fiona is entirely willing to engage with this issue. After all, it is important to her that the fiction is not isolated from real human concerns and also that the fiction is not (in any obvious way) internally inconsistent. An obvious way of avoiding the problem, in principle available both to Reginald and Fiona, is simply to remove, or modify, one of the assumptions generating it. Need God be thought of as being omnipotent and omniscient, for example?

Reginald, however, feels committed to the traditional conception for a number of reasons. First (he explains) the various 'omni' properties, although perhaps not being strictly deducible from the central idea of God as the most perfect being imaginable (or perhaps as so perfect as to transcend the imaginable), nevertheless cohere with that idea. Second, a God with all the 'omni' properties is more worthy of worship than one who lacked these qualities. Third, the explanatory role which God plays in Reginald's ethical world view, in particular God's being the ground of goodness, is not consistent with God's being anything less than perfectly good. Fourth, the explanatory role that God plays in Reginald's metaphysical world view, in particular God's being such that every object and state of affairs depends on him, but not vice versa, requires God's omnipotence. But do these same reasons hold for Fiona? A purely fictional being would not be capable of playing the explanatory role Reginald ascribes to God. A fictional being could not *actually* be the ground of goodness, for example, though it could *fictionally* be that ground. So perhaps Fiona need not be as committed to the traditional conception as Reginald. And perhaps, in any case, the kinds of reason Reginald appeals to could be satisfied by a being which did not exhibit *all* the 'omni' properties. (See, for example, Nagasawa's (2017) presentation and defence of an alternative perfect being theism in terms of a God who has the highest levels of power, knowledge, and so on, that are consistent with each other.)

Whether this strategy really avoids the problem of evil, for either realist or fictionalist, depends on the extent of the modification. Simply allowing God to fall short of perfect power or knowledge, for example, will not be enough. For there are some minimal conditions for whether a being is to count as God, in the religious tradition Reginald stands in. God is the creator of all things, and this implies at least an extraordinary level of power, if not complete omnipotence. God is also a being who cares about creation, and wants the best for it. So there is a divine plan, and that plan must be good, not evil. If this were not the case, then what would be the point of prayer? As we discussed in the previous section, part of the point of prayer – perhaps, indeed, the whole point – is to align one's will with a perfectly good being. If that being were not perfectly good, was indeed flawed, then it would not be a fit object of prayer. Perfect goodness seems the least negotiable of all the 'omni' properties. Now consider this question: would a perfectly good being create a world such as this? Allowing that this being intends to create genuinely free agents, and so cannot know precisely what the outcomes of their free acts will be, it nevertheless should conduct what we now call a *risk assessment* on the creation plan. And even a less than omniscient being, it is reasonable to suppose, would realise that there would be a risk of suffering so terrible that it could not be justified by any good that was likely to result from creation. Admittedly, Reginald does not know this to be the case, but it could, for all he knows, be the case. And so there remains a problem, even with a modification of the assumption of omnipotence and omniscience.

Even though her perspective is very different, Fiona cannot be indifferent to this reasoning. Within the fiction, God is creator, and is also perfectly good. The fiction of a less than perfect God would simply have no useful role to play in her religious outlook. Recall the fictionalist model of prayer as the attempt to align one's will with a perfectly good, loving being. One who is *quite* good, *quite* loving (as long as no-one is making exhausting demands) is just not good or loving enough. So how does one reconcile the decision to create, even given the known risks, with perfect goodness? This version of the problem of evil need not rest on the strong assumptions of the traditional logical problem, so weakening those assumptions does not necessarily make the problem go away. And the problem remains not just for Reginald, but also for Fiona.

4.3 Evading the Problem: an Incomplete Fiction

Eventually, after having considered various theodicies which might make sense of suffering, Reginald proposes that, although there most certainly is a solution to the problem of evil – indeed, must be, for there is both suffering and a loving God – that solution is probably beyond the comprehension of the human mind. Fiona, by exploiting a characteristic feature of standard fiction, can readily agree.

The key feature is this: the kind of fiction we encounter in novels, plays and the like (in other words, the kind of things that announce themselves as fiction) is invariably *incomplete*: some propositions will lack a truth-value within the fiction, since whatever account of truth-in-fiction we adopt, the truth-value of some propositions will be underdetermined by that account. It is entirely indeterminate, for example, whether or not one densely foggy November evening deep in the Scottish Borders country, at a remote mansion known locally merely as 'The Hall', Father Brown (G. K. Chesterton's fictional priest-detective) discovers among the contents of a study – from which a piercing shriek has been heard just as the clock is striking midnight, yet which appears on investigation entirely unoccupied – an umbrella, on the handle of which are inscribed a series of enigmatic runic symbols.... This sentence nowhere appears in any of the Father Brown stories. Nor can it be inferred from the sentences which do. Nor can it be inferred from any plausible reconstruction of the author's intentions. The religious fiction may, indeed will be, similarly incomplete. Among those propositions lacking a truth-value in that fiction may be any statement of a particular theodicy (it is not to be found in any of the canonical writings, but only in interpretative commentaries which lack the fictional authority of those writings – that is, their authority to determine what is true in the fiction). However, the fiction may still be *fictionally complete*: that is, it is fictionally true that, for any proposition, that proposition is either true or false. The fictionalist can entirely consistently, therefore, hold that there *is* a solution to the problem of evil – i.e., that it is true in the fiction that there is such a solution, even if for no specific theodicy T, is T the solution.

The advantage this gives Fiona over Reginald is that she, unlike Reginald, is not committed to the existence of a *particular* successful theodicy, as opposed to the existence of some theodicy or other. Both Reginald and Fiona can agree that all the theodicies they are aware of fall short: they simply fail to make intelligible some of the most horrific instances of suffering they know about. However, for Reginald, there is nevertheless a fact of the matter as to which unknown and perhaps unknowable theodicy is the correct one. And that raises the question: *why* is it impossible for Reginald to grasp this theodicy? For Fiona, in contrast, there is no fact of the matter as to which theodicy is correct. So there is an explanation in Fiona's case as to why she cannot imagine what a satisfactory theodicy would look like – there is nothing for her to imagine!

Ingenious though this approach to the fictionalist problem of evil might be, it is hard to shake off the feeling that it is not so much a solution to the puzzle as a way of dodging it. If Fiona takes this line, she is simply abdicating responsibility for making suffering intelligible within her chosen fiction. All we have here is a religiously empty formula for preventing any conflict between excessive suffering and God. Fiona cannot hope that, buried deep within her fiction, there is some key to the mystery, because such a key would have its source in the human mind (not necessarily Fiona's mind, but in the minds of those who have contributed to the fiction) and part of what is generating the problem is the assumption that no-one has yet come up with a successful theodicy. And yet the fictional fact that there is such a key removes the conflict for Fiona without her ever having engaged with it.

There is a risk, too, that in even positing a successful theodicy within the fiction, without attempting to describe it, the fictionalist is vulnerable to the objection that they are trivialising intense suffering. To suppose that there is a justification for such suffering, the objection goes, is to fail to take it sufficiently seriously. Now it may be that the fictionalist who adopts the strategy outlined here is indeed vulnerable to this objection, but it is not an objection that the religious realist can push, for they are just as vulnerable. It is the kind of objection that is likely to be urged by the anti-theist: one who not only denies the existence of God (traditionally conceived), but also thinks the very idea of God is a bad idea, one we could do without. We are better off, argues the anti-theist, with no God in the world than we would be if such a being really existed. The anti-theist who regards the appeal to God to justify excessive suffering as evil will also regard the fiction that there is some such justification as itself evil.

The fictionalist cannot simply side-step the problem, it seems. The only alternative seems to be to confront it.

4.4 Confronting the Problem: a Paradoxical Fiction

William Hogarth's 1754 engraving, *Satire on False Perspective*, is at first sight simply a busy rural scene featuring an inn, a river with bridge, a hill and church, populated with various characters going about their business: two men fishing, a man in a boat firing a gun, a woman leaning out of the upstairs window of an inn, a walker, some sheep, and so on. A second glance, however, reveals that there is something very wrong: the nearer sheep are smaller than the further sheep, the fishing line of the man in the foreground touches the water beyond that of the more distant fisherman, the woman leaning out of an upstairs window in the nearby inn is able to light the pipe of the walker on the distant hillside, and so on. Although we can interpret the various distance cues individually, we can't interpret them as a group, as they seem to conflict with each other. The fictional world conjured by the painting is a contradictory one, and yet at some level we understand it. Other kinds of contradictions may haunt otherwise intelligible fictions. Consider a time travel story in which the time traveller changes the past. To understand the trip's motivation, we have to accept that a certain event occurred in the past, an event which the traveller regrets and wishes had never taken place. But for the project to be successful, it must turn out that this same event never in fact occurred, thus removing the whole point of the trip. H. G. Wells's short story, *The Man Who Could Work Miracles* (1898), although not explicitly a time travel story, illustrates just this: someone who acquires extraordinary powers comes to regret his use of them, and so seeks to put things back the way they were. Another kind of paradox can be found in stories where one of the characters of a fiction turns out to be the fiction's author. There is nothing paradoxical about an author constructing a fiction about themselves – this happens every time we daydream. What *would* be paradoxical, however, is the idea of a character in a novel revealing themselves to the other characters as the novel's author, and they as his or her creations. Imagine their consternation!

These kinds of case seem importantly different from stories where there is an incidental contradiction, as when the author describes a character as wearing brown shoes at a certain time on page 21 and as wearing black boots at that same time on page 149, where neither type of footwear has any significant conse-quences for the plot. The contradictions above, in contrast, result from aspects of the fiction which are vital to an understanding of what is going on. They also seem importantly different from cases where there are competing and incompatible interpretations of what is going on in a fiction. To take a much-cited example of this phenomenon: are the children in Henry James *The Turn of the Screw* (1898) really under the malevolent influence of the ghosts of Peter Quint and Miss Jessel, or is this all in the young governess's unhinged imagination? Our perspective may shift between these interpretations as we read, but individually the interpretations are consistent: there is no implication that contradiction is internal to the story itself. It might be, rather, that the story is radically indeterminate. In contrast, stories about changing the past, or of a character in a fiction being *within the story* the author of the fiction, appear to be inherently paradoxical. We might attempt to avoid this result by treating such stories as composites of different and consistent fictions, or by providing a consistent interpretation (perhaps time travel stories apparently involving changing the past are actually stories about switching from one time stream to another, each with its distinctive history), but we may feel that something important to the story is lost by these manoeuvres. The point of Hogarth's *False Perspective*, for example, is lost if we see it merely as a fragmented composite, rather than as portraying a single scene. And if we try to resolve the case of the character-author by suggesting that the fiction portrays someone deluded into thinking that they are the author of the fictional events in which they are taking part, then we lose the potential for humour (or horror) that the paradoxical interpretation offers.

After that rather long preamble, let us return to the fictionalist problem of evil. Suppose Fiona wishes to incorporate all of (1)–(6) above into her religious fiction, thus generating a paradox. Could this not be subsumed within the phenomenon we have just identified? Perhaps there is some dramatic benefit to retaining the contradiction rather than seeking to resolve it by means of the artificial manoeuvre outlined in the previous section or some such strategy. Fiona wants to identify with the religious culture of which she is a (perhaps non-standard) part, and that means incorporating within her fiction the 'perfect being' God of one particular Abrahamic tradition. She, like Reginald, feels that the various theodicies on offer fail to explain adequately the depth and extent of suffering on record. Unlike Reginald, however, she feels that *any* theodicy, including ones yet to be articulated, would fail in this way. It is a point of faith for Reginald that there must be such a theodicy, known perhaps only to God. But Fiona feels that any attempt to explain away such evils as have blighted life on Earth would itself be evil. She therefore has to incorporate (6) in her fiction too. And so we have an inescapable contradiction. Fiona's religious fiction is also a paradoxical fiction. The ineradicable clash of ideas has, then, to be part of Fiona's engagement with the fiction. It is something constantly to be struggled with. But this confrontation is, Fiona feels, religiously more satisfactory than any resolution could be.

Jon Robson has suggested that, although inconsistency is undoubtedly an aspect of some fictions, 'inconsistency is not an option for the *religious* fictionalist' (Robson (2015): 356). That, he argues, is because there is a link between religious attitudes and action which is not mirrored by ordinary fiction, and inconsistent narratives could result in inconsistent moral demands. But, as we have already seen, fiction, even religious fiction, cannot *qua fiction* provide reasons for action, except perhaps by revealing the consequences of certain counterfactual scenarios. The mechanism, rather, is indirect, by cultivating certain sensibilities. The presence of paradox in the fiction needs not necessarily undermine that process. As Natalja Deng has put it, 'a story can be both beautiful and inconsistent' (Deng (2015): 206). However, Deng's further point that the fictionalist (at least of the kind we have been pursuing) has no need of a theodicy is perhaps a little too concessive. For an important part of the fiction may be God's own response to suffering, guiding the fictionalist's own.

'Stories may often be paradoxical', says Fiona to Reginald, 'but reality, never.'

Epilogue

The time has come to take stock, pick up a few loose threads, and confess to undefended assumptions.

One rather large undefended assumption was that we can intelligibly draw a contrast between realist and non-realist positions. Not everyone is happy to grant that. D. Z. Phillips, for example, while criticising Braithwaite's view of religious belief as too reductionist (that is, it dispenses with the characteristically religious element), wants to resist the realist/non-realist dichotomy (see, e.g., Phillips (1965), (1988)). I have also assumed, though this has played a less central role in the discussion, that realist positions are at least available in some contexts: one may be a scientific realist but a religious non-realist, for example. But one of the most prominent religious non-realists in modern times, Don Cupitt, defends a much more thoroughgoing non-realism: we construct the world through experience and language (see, e.g., Cupitt (1987), (1991), (2012)). Religious fictionalism is the automatic consequence of global fictionalism. In contrast, much of the motivation briefly sketched in Section 1 for non-realist interpretations of religion is specific to religion, though the problems of meaning and reference may crop up in other areas.

It should be conceded that not all objections to religious realism can be cast simply as objections to the realist component. As Benjamin Cordry (2010) points out, some of the objections to religious world views will carry over to their fictionalist counterparts. Suppose, as Nietzsche said of Christianity, that a religion's view of human nature is demeaning, degrading, or even corrupting (Nietzsche (1895)). Then importing it into a fiction would simply mean that the fiction portrayed human nature in a demeaning, degrading or corrupting way. It might be salutary to immerse oneself in such a fiction for a time, but to make it one's preferred narrative is asking for trouble. The fictionalist naturally, then, will choose as their central religious narrative one with whose values they are in sympathy.

Turning to the problems for religious realism outlined in Section 1, can we come to any provisional conclusions as to how successful fictionalism is in avoiding them? The problem of warrant, surely, will not arise in any straightforward way for the fictionalist. As the religious narrative is not taken by the fictionalist to be objectively fact-stating, they cannot reasonably be asked to cite the evidence on which they suppose it true. Rather, the difficulty will be to work out what it is appropriate to imagine within the fiction, but there, at least, it will be reasonably clear what sources to rely on (a sacred book, for instance), and what those sources say is not so much *evidence* for fictional truth as *constitutive* of it. But what of one aspect of the problem of warrant – the problem of religious diversity? It might be thought that this too is avoided by the fictionalist, since no one religion is being proclaimed as uniquely true. All are in principle available as fictions, and which seem live options will be, in large part, determined by cultural factors. Indeed, one might think that fictionalism was the ideal basis for religious tolerance and pluralism. However, Victoria Harrison (2010) has questioned this. We have been developing the idea of fictionalism as a prescriptive rather than a descriptive theory. But a pluralistic attitude towards religion – one which does not prioritise one religion above others – has to be descriptive, an account of how religious language is in fact used in different traditions. Somehow, it has to be shown that the plethora of actual religious understandings do not come into conflict. And as a descriptive project, Harrison points out, fictionalism would be insensitive to the original purpose of religious discourse (Harrison (2010): 56).

The problem of meaning and the problem of warrant are closely connected for the realist. If, in order to avoid falsification, the realist appeals to the idea of religious language as metaphorical, but also resists the reduction of the metaphorical to the non-metaphorical (and perhaps the non-religious), then there is the question of how we grasp the true meaning of religious assertions. The fictionalist does not need to worry about falsification, so can avoid the proliferation of opaque metaphor. This allows for a more literal interpretation of the terms. And there should be no problem of reference if the fictionalist is only engaged in pretend referring.

The problem of evil, however, does appear to have a counterpart in fictionalism, insofar as the fictionalist includes within the fiction the very ideas which lead to the realist conflict between the idea of God as a perfect being, and the existence of excessive evil which does not seem to be absorbed by existing theodicies. The discussion devoted to this looked at three strategies, two of which seemed inadequate. As for the third: can the fictionalist work with a paradoxical fiction? Whatever the answer to that question, Eleonore Stump (2010) has shown that narrative can be a means of exploring how we might constructively respond to suffering, even if it does not solve the philosophical problems suffering raises for theism.

The other, direct, challenges to fictionalism discussed here had in common the idea that fictionalism is an inadequate basis for full participation in the religious life. There is, for example, the problem of integration into the religious community. However, as Andrew Eshleman (2010) has pointed out, how much of a problem there is here will depend on how the religious community defines itself. Is it primarily in terms of sharing true beliefs about the world, or is it more importantly in terms of shared commitments? As for the issue of whether the fictionalist can engage in such practices as praying, it seems that the fictionalist can appeal to part of the realist's rationale for prayer: that it involves aligning one's will with that of a perfectly loving being, even if that being is merely an imaginative projection.

Two final loose ends before we leave the subject. What is the connection between religious fictionalism and agnosticism? Could the religious agnostic also adopt non–truth-normed attitudes to religious statements in living a religious life? Perhaps, and indeed proponents of non-doxasticism appear to be exploring just this possibility, but the difference between this and the kind of fictionalism we have been discussing is the latter gives *pretence* and *make-believe* a key role. And this links with the second loose end, which promises to be a fruitful line of enquiry. It is to do with the psychology of fiction. Is there something about fictionality, and the ways in which we orient ourselves towards fiction, that might put the fictionalist at an advantage over the realist? Perhaps, by raising challenging and potentially unsettling matters in a safe environment (fiction cannot directly endanger us), fiction can focus our attention on the morally salient issues, without the distracting complexity of reality. Or is this just escapism?

We will have to leave it there for now, but I hope that enough has been said to show how rash it would be to assume that, to adapt a remark by C. S. Lewis, a religion, if false, is of no importance.

Glossary

What follows are definitions of key terms as they are used in this book, organised for the most part in terms of definitional priority rather than alphabetically. That is, the basic ideas are presented first, followed by ideas which can be defined in terms of those already presented.

Statement: An indicative sentence, one whose form suggests that it is representing things as being a certain way, such as 'The sun is shining', a form suitable for making assertions.

Truth-apt: An attitude or sentence is *truth-apt* if it is capable of being true or false. This applies, for example, to beliefs and assertions, but not, e.g., to commands, desires or expressions of hope.

Truth-normed: An attitude or statement is *truth-normed* if it is answerable to how things are. That is, its truth, or assumed truth, is an essential part of what makes that attitude or statement appropriate. Belief is truth-normed, pretence is not.

Irreducible: A statement concerning a certain subject matter (such as values, or numbers, or scientific theoretical entities, or religious objects) is *irreducible* if it cannot be replaced by a sentence which has a different subject matter without loss of factual content. The *factual content* of a sentence is given by the conditions which would have to obtain if that sentence is to be true.

Objectively fact-stating: A statement is *objectively fact-stating* if its intended purpose is to say something about the world as it is independently of our beliefs, attitudes or conventions about the subject matter of that sentence.

Realism: A view of the nature and function of a certain language or area of discourse, such as moral, mathematical, scientific, or religious discourse. Realism concerning a language holds the following tenets about statements in the language:

(i)   They are *truth-apt*;
(ii)   They are *irreducible*;
(iii)   Their purpose is to be *objectively fact-stating*.

Cognitive/non-cognitive: An attitude is *cognitive* if it represents things as being a certain way, and so is answerable to how things are. Beliefs are cognitive attitudes; hopes, emotions, and sentiments of approval are non-cognitive.

Religious realism: The *religious realist* takes realism about religious language to be essential to their engagement with the religious life (and perhaps to anyone's authentic engagement with the religious life).The **doxastic religious realist** (doxasticist) holds in addition that religious statements express *belief in* the truth of those statements. The **non-doxastic religious realist** (non-doxasticist) holds that religious statements can express some kind of acceptance which represents a lower kind of commitment than does belief.

We can define non-realist positions in terms of which of the tenets of realism they accept and which they reject:

Expressivism: Rejects (i), (ii) and (iii) of the realist's tenets. Statements in the given language are not fact-stating and so are neither true nor false. Rather (when used in particular occasions), they express certain non-cognitive attitudes. Different forms of expressivism will appeal to different non-cognitive attitudes. **Affective expressionism** about religious statements holds that such statements express emotional feelings – for example, feelings of love, or awe or reverence. **Conative expressivism** about religious statements holds that they express commitment to certain kinds of action. (What are sometimes called 'moderate attitude' theories take religious statements to express both cognitive and non-cognitive attitudes.)

Positivism: Accepts (i) but denies (ii) and (iii) of the realist's tenets. Statements in the given language are capable of being true or false but are equivalent in terms of factual content to statements in a different language, and in particular (because historically influenced by *verificationism* (q.v.)), a language which primarily concerns experience. So, e.g., scientific positivism takes scientific theoretical statements to be replaceable by observation statements with no theoretical content. Similarly, positivism about religious statements takes such religious statements as replaceable by statements with no overt religious content, such as statements about certain kinds of experiences. So the statements in the given language are fact-stating, but the facts are not independent of our attitudes about the world.

Fictionalism: The central thesis of fictionalism concerning a language or area of discourse is that acceptance of statements in that language is not, or need not be, *truth-normed*: that is, such acceptance is not, or need not be, vindicated by the actual truth of those statements; they may be useful or valuable in some other way. That attitude, however, might be paired up with more than one view of the nature and function of the statements in question. One might, for instance, be a realist about scientific theoretical statements, and yet think that their truth is not what matters. What matters may be their usefulness in predicting phenomena, and it is this usefulness that vindicates commitment to those statements. But equally, one might think that acceptance of the statements is not truth-normed because they are fictional statements: what matters is not their actual truth but their *fictional* truth. If they are being used, not simply to describe the content of a fiction, but as part of an active engagement with that fiction, the associated attitude is one of pretence.

Religious fictionalism: In this Element, I have used the term to denote a theory of religious language that accepts (i) and (ii) but denies (iii) of the realist tenets with respect to religious language. Religious statements are made in a context of make-believe. A fictionalist who says 'The world was created by God' as part of the game of make-believe is *pretending* to assert, not actually asserting, that the world was created by God. They are capable of being true (or false), but they are only true (or false) within a specific fiction. They are fact-stating, but the facts they state, because fictional, are not attitude- or convention-independent.

Verificationism: A theory about what is required for statements in general to be meaningful, sometimes supplemented by a theory of the meaning of statements. The central tenet of verificationism is the *principle of verifiability*: a statement is factually meaningful (succeeds in saying something intelligible about the world) if, and only if, it can be verified, or at least confirmed, by experience. An arguably stronger principle is that the meaning of an assertoric statement is given in terms of the possible experiences which would verify it. Verification, in most contexts, forces a move away from realism towards some form of non-realism (historically, positivism, which would now generally be regarded as the least attractive form of non-realism).

Descriptive/prescriptive distinction: All the above theories concerning a language can be understood in one of two ways: *descriptively* or *prescriptively*. A **descriptive** theory attempts to capture what views people actually have towards a particular topic. A **prescriptive** theory puts forward a proposal as to what view people ought to have. In some recent literature on fictionalism, the view that people are in fact fictionalists about a particular subject matter is described as *hermeneutic fictionalism*; the view that people ought to be fictionalists about that subject matter is described as *revolutionary fictionalism*. Our concern has mainly been with the latter.

Table of positions in realism/non-realism debates

Are the sentences in the discourse	Realism	Fictionalism	Positivism	Expressivism
truth-apt?	Yes	Yes	Yes	No
irreducible?	Yes	Yes	No	No
(intended to be) objectively fact-stating?	Yes	No	No	No

Bibliography

The following contains items referred to in the text, but also some recent writings which, for reasons of space, I have not been able to discuss, but to which the reader is directed.

Arnold, Matthew (1884). *Literature and Dogma*, London: Smith, Elder & Co.

Ayer, A. J. (1936). *Language, Truth and Logic*, London: Victor Gollancz; second edition, reprinted, Penguin Books London: Penguin, 1971.

(1946). Preface to second edition of *Language, Truth and Logic*, London: Victor Gollancz; reprinted, Penguin Books, London: Penguin, 1971.

Basinger, David (1983). 'Why Petition an Omnipotent, Omniscient, Wholly Good God?', *Religious Studies* 19: 25–42.

Braithwaite, R. B. (1955). 'An Empiricist's View of the Nature of Religious Belief', Ninth Arthur Stanley Edington Lecture, reprinted in Mitchell (1971): 72–91.

Brock, Stuart, and Mares, Edwin (2007). *Realism and Anti-Realism*, Durham: Acumen

Byrne, Peter (2003). *God and Realism*, Aldershot: Ashgate.

Chesterton, G. K. (1916). 'Introduction to the Book of Job'; reprinted in *The Chesterton Review* 11 (1985): 5–15.

Coakley, Sarah (2002). 'What Does Chalcedon Solve and What Is it Not? Some Reflections on the Status and Meaning of the Chalcedonian "Definition"', in Davis, Stephen T., Kendall, Daniel, and O'Collins, Daniel, eds., *The Incarnation*, Oxford: Oxford University Press (2002): 143–63.

Cordry, Benjamin S. (2010). 'A Critique of Religious Fictionalism', *Religious Studies* 46: 77–89.

Cupitt, Don (1980). *Taking Leave of God*, London: SCM Press.

(1987). *The Long-Legged Fly*, London: SCM Press.

(1991). *What Is a Story?* London: SCM Press.

(2012). *The Last Testament*, London: SCM Press.

Currie, Gregory (1990). *The Nature of Fiction*, Cambridge: Cambridge University Press.

Davidson, Donald (1963). 'Actions, Reasons and Causes', in *Essays on Actions and Events*, Oxford: Clarendon Press, 1982: 3–19.

Dawkins, Richard (2006). *The God Delusion*, London: Black Swan.

Deng, Natalja (2015). 'Religion for Naturalists', *International Journal for the Philosophy of Religion* 78: 195–214.

Eddington, Arthur (1939). *The Philosophy of Physical Science*, Cambridge: Cambridge University Press.

Eklund, Matti (2015). 'Fictionalism', *Stanford Encyclopedia of Philosophy*, https://plato.stanford.edu/entries/fictionalism/.

Eshleman, Andrew (2005). 'Can an Atheist Believe in God?', *Religious Studies* 41: 183–99.

    (2010). 'Religious Fictionalism Defended: Reply to Cordry', *Religious Studies* 46: 91–6.

    (2016). 'The Afterlife: beyond Belief', *International Journal for Philosophy of Religion* 82 (2): 163–83.

Field, Hartry (1980). *Science without Numbers*, Princeton: Princeton University Press.

Flew, Antony, and MacIntyre, Alasdair eds. (1955). *New Essays in Philosophical Theology*, London: SCM Press.

Forrest, Peter (1997). 'The Epistemology of Religion', *Stanford Encyclopedia of Philosophy*, https://plato.stanford.edu/entries/religion-epistemology/.

Gender, Tamar Szabo (2008). 'Alief and Belief', *Journal of Philosophy* 105: 634–63.

Grice, H. P. (1957). 'Meaning', *Philosophical Review* 66: 377–88.

Hacking, Ian (1983). *Representing and Intervening*, Cambridge: Cambridge University Press.

Harrison, Victoria (2010). 'Philosophy of Religion, Fictionalism, and Religious Diversity', *International Journal for the Philosophy of Religion* 68: 43–58.

Hick, John (1960). 'Theology and Verification', reprinted in Mitchell (1971): 53–71.

    (2007). *Evil and the God of Love*, 2nd ed., London: Macmillan.

    (1989). *An Interpretation of Religion*, London: Macmillan.

Hitchens, Christopher (2007). *God Is Not Great: How Religion Poisons Everything*, New York: Hachette Book Group.

Howard-Snyder, Daniel (2013). 'Schellenberg on Propositional Faith', *Religious Studies* 49 (2): 181–94.

    (2019). 'Can Fictionalists Have Faith? It All Depends', *Religious Studies* 55.

Hume, David (1757). 'Of Tragedy', in Green, T. H. and Grose, T. H. *The Philosophical Works of David Hume*, London: Longman, Green (1874–75), Vol. 3.

Jay, Christopher (2014). 'The Kantian Moral Hazard Argument for Religious Fictionalism', *International Journal for the Philosophy of Religion* 68: 43–58.

64 Bibliography

Joyce, Richard (2005). 'Moral Fictionalism', in Kalderon (2005): 287–313.

Kalderon, Mark Eli ed. (2005). *Fictionalism in Metaphysics*, Oxford: Clarendon Press.

Kodaj, Daniel (2014). 'The Problem of Religious Evil', *Religious Studies* 50 (4): 425–43.

Kripke, Saul (1972). *Naming and Necessity*, Oxford: Blackwell.

Lamarque, Peter (1981). 'How Can We Fear and Pity Fictions?', *British Journal of Aesthetics* 21 (4): 291–304.

Leslie, John (1989) *Universes*, London: Routledge.

Lewis, C. S. (1955). *Surprised by Joy*, London: Bles.

Lipton, Peter (2007). 'Science and Religion: the Immersion Solution', in Moore and Scott (2007): 31–46.

McBrayer, J. (2010). 'Skeptical Theism,' *Philosophy Compass* 4 (1): 1–13.

Mackie, J. L. (1977). *Ethics: Inventing Right and Wrong*, London: Penguin.

(1982). *The Miracle of Theism*, Oxford: Clarendon Press.

Malcolm, Finlay (2018). 'Can Fictionalists Have Faith?', *Religious Studies* 54: 215–32.

Malcolm, Finlay, and Scott, Michael (2017). 'Faith, Belief and Fictionalism', *Pacific Philosophical Quarterly* 98: 257–74.

(2018) 'Religious Fictionalism', *Philosophy Compass* 13: 1–11.

Matravers, Derek (1997). 'The Paradox of Fiction: the Report versus the Perceptual Model', in Hjort, Mette and Laver, Sue eds. *Emotion and the Arts*. Oxford: Oxford University Press: 78–92.

Mitchell, Basil ed. (1971), *The Philosophy of Religion*, Oxford: Oxford University Press.

Moore, Andrew, and Scott, Michael, eds. (2007). *Realism and Religion: Philosophical and Theological Perspectives*, Aldershot: Ashgate.

Nagasawa, Yujin (2017). *Maximal God*, Oxford: Oxford University Press.

Newton-Smith, W. H. (1981). *The Rationality of Science*, London: Routledge & Kegan Paul.

Nietzsche, Friedrich (1895). *The Anti-Christ*, in *Twilight of the Idols and the Anti-Christ*, translated by R. J. Hollingdale, Harmondsworth: Penguin.

Phillips, D. Z. (1965). *The Concept of Prayer*, London: Routledge & Kegan Paul.

(1988) *Faith after Foundationalism*, London: Routledge.

Plantinga, Alvin (1977). *God, Freedom and Evil*, Grand Rapids, MI: Eerdmans.

Pojman, Louis (1986). 'Faith without Belief', *Faith and Philosophy* 3: 157–76.

Radford, Colin (1975). 'How Can We Moved By the Fate of Anna Karenina?', *Proceedings of the Aristotelian Society* Supplementary Volume 49: 67–80.

Robson, Jon (2015). 'Religious Fictionalism and the Problem of Evil', *Religious Studies* 51: 535–60.

Rosen, Gideon (1990). 'Modal Fictionalism', *Mind* 99: 327–54.

Rowe, William L. (1978). *Philosophy of Religion: An Introduction*, Encino, CA: Dickenson Publishing Company.

Sauchelli, Andrea (2018). 'The Will to Make-Believe: Religious Fictionalism, Religious Beliefs, and the Value of Art, *Philosophy and Phenomenological Research* 96: 620–35.

Schaper, Eva (1978). 'Fiction and the Suspension of Disbelief', *British Journal of Aesthetics* 18 (1): 31–44.

Scott, Michael (2000). 'Framing the Realism Question', *Religious Studies* 36 (4): 455–71.

(2013). *Religious Language*, Basingstoke: Palgrave Macmillan.

(2017). 'Religious Language', *Stanford Encyclopedia of Philosophy*, https:// plato.stanford.edu/entries/religious-language/.

Soskice, Janet (1987). *Metaphor and Religious Language*, Oxford: Clarendon Press.

Stump, Eleonore (2010). *Wandering in Darkness: Narrative and the Problem of Suffering*, Oxford: Clarendon Press.

Swinburne, Richard (1977). *The Coherence of Theism*, Oxford: Clarendon Press.

van Fraassen, Bas (1980). *The Scientific Image*, Oxford: Clarendon Press.

Walton, Kendal (1978). 'Fearing Fictions', *Journal of Philosophy* 65: 5–27.

White, Roger (2010). *Talking About God: The Concept of Analogy and the Problem of Religious Language*, Farnham: Ashgate.

Acknowledgements

I am very grateful to Yujin Nagasawa, for commissioning this Element, and for encouragement, and to an anonymous reader for very helpful comments on an earlier draft.

For Don Cupitt

Philosophy of Religion

Yujin Nagasawa

University of Birmingham

Yujin Nagasawa is Professor of Philosophy and Co-Director of the John Hick Centre for Philosophy of Religion at the University of Birmingham. He is currently President of the British Society for the Philosophy of Religion. He is a member of the Editorial Board of *Religious Studies*, the *International Journal for Philosophy of Religion* and *Philosophy Compass*.

About the Series

This Cambridge Elements series provides concise and structured introductions to all the central topics in the philosophy of religion. It offers balanced, comprehensive coverage of multiple perspectives in the philosophy of religion. Contributors to the series are cutting-edge researchers who approach central issues in the philosophy of religion. Each provides a reliable resource for academic readers and develops new ideas and arguments from a unique viewpoint.

Cambridge Elements ☰

Philosophy of Religion

A full series listing is available at: www.cambridge.org/EPREL

Made in the USA
Middletown, DE
12 December 2022